Vagus Nerve Exercises

Relieve Anxiety, Support Trauma Recovery, Calm Inflammation, Improve Digestion and Sleep, and Reset Your Nervous System Naturally

Hector Rivera, RN, BSN

HARZ
Publishing, LLC

Harz Publishing LLC

Disclaimer & Terms of Use

ISBN: 978-1-969577-25-3 (eBook)

ISBN: 978-1-969577-26-0 (Paperback)

ISBN: 978-1-969577-27-7 (Hardcover)

Preface

I DIDN'T WRITE THIS book to add more noise to your life. I wrote it because, at some point, you may have realized something wasn't working. Maybe your body feels tense for no clear reason. Maybe your thoughts don't slow down, even when you try to rest. Or maybe you've tried different approaches—medication, therapy, routines—and still feel like something is missing.

That's where the vagus nerve comes in.

You don't need to understand every detail of neuroscience to benefit from this work. What matters is learning to work with your body rather than against it. The vagus nerve helps regulate how your body handles stress, supports digestion, influences sleep, and shapes your emotional state. When it's supported, your system begins to shift out of constant alertness and into a calmer, more stable state.

This book focuses on simple, practical exercises you can use in real life. Not perfect conditions. Not long routines. Just small, repeatable actions that help your body feel safer and more regulated over time.

You won't find complicated systems here. You'll find breathing techniques, gentle movement, sensory practices, and short resets you can use throughout your day—even when life feels busy or overwhelming.

Some of these exercises may feel subtle at first. That's normal. Real change in the nervous system often starts quietly—a slower breath, a moment of ease, a slight shift in tension. Over time, those small changes build.

You don't need to do everything in this book. You don't need to do it perfectly. What matters is showing up, even in small ways, and giving your body consistent signals of safety.

If you've felt stuck, overwhelmed, or disconnected from your own body, this is a place to begin again—without pressure.

Take what helps. Leave what doesn't. Come back when you need to.

That's enough.

Contents

Introduction

YOU WAKE UP ALREADY tired. Your mind starts racing before your feet even hit the floor. Your chest feels tight, your stomach uneasy, and even small problems feel overwhelming. For many people, this becomes the normal rhythm of daily life. Stress lingers in the background, sleep never feels fully restorative, and the body rarely gets a chance to truly relax.

Many people live this way for years without realizing their nervous system remains in survival mode. Anxiety, digestive problems, poor sleep, chronic inflammation, and emotional exhaustion often share the same hidden root: a nervous system that no longer knows how to shift easily between stress and calm.

My name is Hector Rivera. I am a registered nurse and an author. Still, more importantly, I am someone who understands how deeply anxiety, trauma, and chronic stress can affect a person's life.

During my work in hospitals and mental health facilities, I have seen first-hand how these struggles affect patients and their families. I have watched people deal with sleepless nights, persistent pain, and emotions that refuse to settle. I have listened to stories filled with frustration and fear as people wonder whether lasting relief is even possible.

These experiences also connect to my own life. Like many people, I have gone through periods of trauma, anxiety, and long nights without sleep. Living through those moments helped me see more clearly how closely the mind and body are connected. It also encouraged me to explore practical ways people can support their nervous system and overall well-being.

This book begins with an exploration of the science behind the vagus nerve and its significance. You'll find self-assessments to help you better understand your nervous system, followed by clear, practical exercises—adaptable for individuals with trauma or chronic illness. We'll also cover how to build routines, overcome standard blocks, and stay consistent. In the final chapters, you'll get tools and resources to support long-term healing.

Quick Start Guide: Begin Here

How to Use This Book

You don't need to read this book perfectly or follow every exercise at once. Many readers start with the Quick Start routines and then explore the chapters that speak most to their symptoms—whether that's anxiety, digestion, sleep, or trauma recovery. Move at your own pace. Even small, consistent steps can help your nervous system learn a new rhythm.

If you're eager to get started, these three beginner-friendly routines are safe, gentle, and effective. No prep is needed—just you and a few quiet minutes.

These are just a few gentle exercises to get you started. You'll find more detailed instructions, science, and variations in the chapters ahead. For now, try what feels doable.

Routine 1: Breath Reset

1. Sit or lie comfortably.
2. Inhale through your nose for four seconds.
3. Hold the breath for four seconds.
4. Slowly breathe out through your mouth for about six seconds.
5. Repeat for two to three minutes.

Tip: If counting feels stressful, simply focus on making the exhale longer than the inhale.

Routine 2: Humming & Grounding

- Sit with feet flat on the floor.
- Hum gently on your exhale, like a soft "mmmm."
- Place one hand on your chest or belly.
- Repeat for 1 minute.

Routine 3: Cold & Calm

- Splash cold water on your face or press a cool cloth to your cheeks and eyes.
- Take 3 slow breaths while doing so.
- Feel your body begin to settle.

This book is not about doing everything perfectly. It's about finding what works for you at your own pace. You do not have to do this alone. I created this book to walk with you every step of the way.

You have already demonstrated courage by seeking answers. I invite you to begin a new chapter—one where calm, healing, and wellness are within your reach. The path starts here, and this book is here to guide you through that process.

Note to the reader: If you've read my other somatic books, some exercises or ideas may feel familiar. I designed each book to stand on its own while focusing on a specific area of healing.

Chapter 1

Demystifying the Vagus Nerve: Your Built-In Healing Pathway

You might not realize it, but there's a part of your body quietly working behind the scenes, shaping how you feel from the moment you wake up to the second your head hits the pillow.

A woman named Lila had spent years feeling like her body was working against her. She dealt with stomach pain that appeared at the worst times, a racing heart that kept her on edge, and a constant exhaustion that never fully lifted—no matter how many treatments or diets she tried.

Lila often felt lost in her own body, as if there were a hidden switch she couldn't find. What she didn't know was that this "switch" was real. It exists in all of us, and it's called the vagus nerve.

If you've struggled with anxiety, trauma, gut issues, or poor sleep, this chapter will show you why the vagus nerve matters to you.

The Vagus Nerve Decoded: What It Is and Why It Matters

The vagus nerve is not just any nerve. It's the longest cranial nerve in the human body, stretching from your brainstem down through your neck and chest, then weaving its way into your heart, lungs, stomach, and intestines.

The term "vagus" comes from Latin, meaning "wandering"—a fitting name for a nerve that travels from your brain to your abdomen, connecting with nearly every major organ along the way. You have two vagus nerves, one on each side of your body, acting as the body's "communication superhighway."

What makes the vagus nerve unique is its broad influence throughout the body. Unlike many nerves that serve a single function, the vagus nerve helps regulate several vital processes at once, including heart rate, breathing, digestion, and even aspects of vocal tone. As a key part of the parasympathetic nervous system, it plays a central role in rest, recovery, and healing—working automatically in the background without requiring conscious effort.

Now, why does this matter for anxiety, trauma, inflammation, digestion, and sleep? Because the vagus nerve acts as a regulator—a kind of "brake pedal" for your entire system. When it's working well, it calms your stress response and invites healing back into your body.

Think about what happens during a panic attack or a stressful argument. Your heart pounds, your breath shortens, your stomach tightens, and maybe you start sweating or shaking. That's your body's alarm system firing up. The vagus nerve holds the power to quiet this alarm—to slow things down and return you to a state where you can think clearly and feel safe again.

The influence doesn't stop there. The vagus nerve also helps control inflammation throughout your body. When this nerve sends strong signals, it can actually "dial down" inflammation—something scientists call the "cholinergic anti-inflammatory pathway." On nights when sleep evades you or mornings when your joints ache for no apparent reason, this silent operator might be struggling to do its job.

Digestive issues? The vagus nerve tells your gut when to move food along or rest. If its signals get scrambled by stress or trauma, symptoms like bloating or pain often follow.

I know medical talk can get overwhelming, so let's ground this with an analogy. Think of your body as a busy city with neighborhoods representing different organs—your heart is downtown, your gut is midtown, and your lungs are uptown. The vagus nerve is like a fleet of subway trains running day and night, delivering messages between various parts of the body. If the trains run smoothly, the city thrives; if they stall or break down, chaos erupts.

This 'reset button' isn't abstract—it's real. We all have moments when we wish we could pause on stress or pain. The vagus nerve is nature's way of giving you that ability. You don't need gadgets or complicated routines—just awareness and a few practical tools.

In this book, you'll learn how to tap into your vagus nerve's potential using simple exercises—tools that help your body recover its balance and resilience. You'll see how this "wandering nerve" can transform frustration into hope by providing a clear path out of overwhelm and into calm, self-regulated behavior.

The "Rest-and-Digest" Switch: How the Vagus Nerve Soothes Your Body

Imagine you're walking down a dark street at night and hear footsteps behind you. Your breath shortens, and your muscles tense—your body reacting to stress.

While the fight-or-flight response is helpful in emergencies, your vagus nerve plays the opposite role. It signals your system to slow down, recover, and return to a calm state. In today's world, stress isn't always loud or obvious, but your vagus nerve helps reset the alarm so your body can feel safe again.

Now, picture the opposite. You settle into a soft chair with a warm cup of tea. Your breathing slows, your shoulders drop, and a sense of ease begins to settle in.

When the vagus nerve activates, your body shifts into its natural "rest-and-digest" mode. This signal tells your heart to slow down, your breath to deepen, and your gut to return to a state of calm function. It's not just relaxation—it's full-body restoration. When your vagus nerve is engaged, your body receives a clear message: it's safe to let go, to digest, to heal, and to rest.

For many people today, this calming state feels distant. Stress rarely disappears; it lingers in the background as muscle tension, digestive problems, restless nights, or sudden waves of anxiety.

Modern life rarely allows true pauses. Notifications interrupt dinner, news cycles never stop, and past trauma can keep the body locked in a state of constant alertness.

We get stuck with the stress switch jammed on, unable to find our way back to calm. The result is burnout, chronic inflammation, mood swings, and a body that feels like it's running on fumes.

That's when vagus nerve exercises can make a real difference. They're not just another item on a wellness checklist or a passing trend. They offer practical, body-based tools to help you shift out of survival mode—especially when your system can't do it on its own.

Think of these exercises as giving your nervous system a "manual override." You can teach yourself to find the brake pedal and slow everything down—even when life is loud and overwhelming. It's more than just telling yourself to relax; it's learning how to send real signals that reach every organ and cell.

When you activate "rest-and-digest" mode with purpose, everything changes. Breathing evens out. Your heart finds its natural rhythm instead of racing ahead. Digestion improves—you might finally feel hungry at mealtimes or notice less bloating after eating. Muscles relax their grip on tension that's been there for years. You start sleeping more deeply and waking up refreshed rather than groggy and achy. The mind quiets its chatter; worries lose their grip; setbacks don't knock you down as hard. Minor problems feel manageable instead of overwhelming.

What's most remarkable is how this state builds resilience for the future. Each time you practice shifting into calm, you strengthen the pathways that make returning to baseline easier next time. It's like forging a new trail in the woods—at first, it's wild and tangled, but with repetition, the way becomes smooth and familiar. Over time, your body learns what safety feels like again and begins to trust that it can get there, no matter what life throws at you.

For those who have lived through trauma or relentless stress, this is not just physical relief—it's emotional repair. You no longer have to feel trapped in old reactions or helpless against panic or pain flares. The vagus nerve gives you a fundamental tool for changing your experience from the inside out. With regular practice, you'll find yourself facing challenges with steadier hands and a quieter mind.

If you want a quick check-in right now, pause and notice your breath and your heartbeat. Is your breathing fast or slow? Is your heartbeat fast or slow? Are you clenching your jaw or shoulders? These small cues are your nervous system talking to you—and with the help of simple vagus nerve exercises, you'll soon learn that you have the power to shift those cues toward calm and comfort whenever you need it most.

Polyvagal Theory in Plain English: Understanding Your Body's Safety Modes

If you've ever wondered why your reactions sometimes feel out of your control—why you freeze during a tough conversation, find your mind foggy in stressful moments, or feel oddly numb instead of anxious—polyvagal theory can offer some real answers.

Developed by Dr. Stephen Porges, this framework shines a light on how your nervous system decides, second by second, whether you are safe, under threat, or at risk of complete overwhelm. In simple terms, polyvagal theory explains why the body may react with anxiety, shutdown, or connection even before the conscious mind fully understands what is happening.

Your nervous system is constantly scanning the world for signals. Think of it as a built-in security system, always evaluating whether it is safe to open up, defend itself, or disconnect to survive.

Polyvagal theory breaks your experience down into three primary states. The first is the social engagement mode—sometimes called the "safe and connected" state. In this state, you feel grounded and able to talk, laugh, make eye contact, and trust others. Your breathing is steady, your voice is clear, and digestion works as it should—the ventral branch of the vagus nerve powers this state.

The second state is the classic fight-or-flight response. Here, the body prepares for action. Heart rate rises, muscles tense, and thoughts may begin to race. You might feel irritable, restless, or panicky as your system shifts into protection mode.

When neither connection nor active defense feels possible, the third state appears: shutdown or freeze. Powered by the dorsal branch of the vagus nerve, this mode can leave you foggy, disconnected, numb, or overwhelmingly tired. It's the nervous system's way of pulling the plug when things feel truly unsafe. Some people describe it as watching life from behind a glass wall.

Two branches of the vagus nerve help shape these states: the ventral branch and the dorsal branch. Each plays a different role in how your nervous system responds to safety, stress, or overwhelm.

The ventral vagal branch is like a friendly neighbor—it promotes feelings of safety and supports social connection. Imagine sitting at a family dinner where you feel welcomed and heard. Your heart feels calm, laughter comes easily, and digestion works smoothly. In moments like these, the ventral vagal system is running the show.

Now, picture public speaking in front of a crowd. Your palms sweat, your voice shakes, and your stomach tightens. That's your nervous system shifting toward a fight-or-flight response as your body senses possible danger.

The dorsal branch acts more like an emergency power-down. When life feels too overwhelming, and escape seems impossible, it steps in to conserve energy and protect you. You might notice this after a long day of stress—perhaps stuck in traffic with a pounding headache, first feeling irritated, then suddenly exhausted or spaced out.

This shutdown response isn't just a theory—it shows up in daily life all the time. Take anxiety attacks, for example. When stress builds—whether from constant work pressure or unresolved trauma—your body can flip into fight-or-flight mode at the slightest trigger: a ringing phone or a sharp word from your boss. Your heart rockets, your breathing turns shallow, and your mind floods with worry.

At other times, especially after significant traumas or repeated stressors, the nervous system chooses a different route: shutdown. You might find yourself staring blankly at the TV for hours or sleeping all day, unable to muster energy or emotion. Numbness replaces panic—not because you don't care anymore but because your body sees checking out as safer than feeling everything at once.

I've seen this pattern countless times—people struggling with anxiety, feeling broken because they overreact or lose control of their moods.

If this pattern feels familiar, I want you to know something important: these responses are not character flaws or personal failings. They are ancient survival strategies deeply ingrained in your biology. Your nervous system isn't out to sabotage you; it's doing its best to protect you with the resources it has available.

Every time you find yourself snapping at someone you love or zoning out during an important meeting, it's not a weakness—it's your internal alarm system flipping switches to keep you safe based on what it senses about the world.

Once you understand these modes, many of your reactions start to make a lot more sense. When you start to recognize which state you're in—social engagement, fight-or-flight, or shutdown—you gain a new kind of control. You can learn to "work with" your nervous system instead of fighting against it. You see that irritability doesn't mean you're a bad parent or partner; numbness isn't laziness; panic isn't madness. It's all your body's way of saying: "I'm trying to help."

When you recognize these patterns, you respond with compassion instead of shame—and you start using techniques that work with your body's natural ability to heal and reconnect.

The Gut-Brain Connection: How the Vagus Nerve Affects Digestion and Mood

Every day life often reminds us how closely the gut and mind are connected. Think about the times when a difficult conversation left you with "butterflies in your stomach," or when a wave of anxiety made your stomach churn. These expressions aren't just poetic phrases—they reflect the real communication happening between your brain and your digestive system.

The primary messenger in this ongoing conversation is the vagus nerve. It carries signals back and forth between the brain and many organs, especially the digestive system.

When stress rises, the brain sends signals through this nerve to the gut, telling it to slow or pause digestion. As a result, digestion may stall, leading to bloating, cramps, or nausea.

Communication also flows the other way. When the gut is inflamed or irritated—such as with IBS, food sensitivities, or chronic digestive pain—it can send signals back to the brain, sometimes increasing feelings of worry, tension, or low mood.

It has become clear that gut health does more than handle food; it also influences how you feel emotionally. If you've ever noticed feeling low when your digestion is off or irritable when you're bloated or uncomfortable, you've experienced the gut-brain axis at work. This connection runs deeper than most people realize. The vagus nerve doesn't just carry information from the brain to the belly—it also relays updates from the gut back to the brain. Approximately 80% of its fibers travel upward, carrying information about nutrient status, inflammation, and the balance of gut bacteria. In other words, your "gut feelings" are real—your body's way of keeping your mind in the loop about what's happening internally.

For anyone struggling with digestive problems like IBS, chronic bloating, or random bouts of stomach pain, the vagus nerve's role becomes especially important. When your body stays stuck in stress mode for too long—maybe because of trauma, burnout, or relentless anxiety—your gut gets the signal to clamp down. Stress can reduce blood flow to the stomach and intestines, reduce the release of digestive enzymes, and slow the digestive process.

Symptoms flare up, including pain after meals, unpredictable bathroom trips, or constant discomfort that makes daily life harder than it needs to be. Over time, this can create a harmful loop—gut discomfort heightens anxious thoughts, and those thoughts further disrupt digestion.

The impact goes beyond the stomach—gut health often drives mood disorders like anxiety and depression in ways that surprise people. When inflammation lingers in the gut, it can trigger shifts in brain chemistry, sometimes amplifying negative thoughts or making it harder to shake off feelings of sadness. People recovering from trauma often battle both emotional highs and lows and unpredictable digestion at the same time. The two are rarely separate; they dance together, sometimes making a recovery feel out of reach.

What's promising is that research is beginning to show that activating the vagus nerve may help interrupt this cycle. Vagus nerve stimulation—sending signals purposefully along this nerve—has been linked to improvements in both mood and digestive symptoms.

Some studies suggest that gentle techniques that stimulate the vagus nerve can reduce bloating and abdominal pain in people with IBS while also improving overall well-being. Researchers believe this occurs because vagal activation can help calm gut inflammation and restore healthy communication between the brain and the digestive system.

For people dealing with anxiety or depression alongside digestive problems, these practices may offer additional support. They don't replace medical care, but they can complement treatments such as medication, nutrition changes, or therapy.

You might wonder if all this means you need special gadgets or endless appointments with specialists. The answer is no. Soon, you'll discover practical methods—simple breathing patterns, vocal exercises, gentle movement—that engage your vagus nerve right at home. These aren't complicated tricks; they're straightforward tools that give you back a sense of control over your symptoms. You'll learn how to "hack" the gut-brain connection for yourself, calming an upset stomach before a big meeting or easing anxiety that comes out of nowhere.

As you work through these strategies in later chapters, you'll notice changes—not just in your digestion or energy but in how steady and resilient you feel each day. The power to shift both mood and gut health isn't far off; it's already built into your body, waiting for you to tap into it.

Common Myths and FAQs: Busting Vagus Nerve Misconceptions

It's understandable to be skeptical when hearing that simple vagus nerve exercises might help with anxiety, trauma, digestion, or sleep—especially after years of searching for solutions. You may wonder: "Is this just another wellness fad?" or "Why didn't my doctor mention this?" These are valid questions, and it's important to sort fact from fiction.

One prevailing myth is that vagus nerve exercises are just another fleeting trend. The truth is that the vagus nerve has been recognized by medicine for over a century, primarily in the fields of neurology and surgery. What's new is our recent awareness of its role in everyday health outside the clinic.

Doctors have long used medical devices to stimulate the vagus nerve for certain conditions like epilepsy or depression. What's changing is an increased understanding that you can influence the vagus nerve at home—no surgery or expensive tools are required.

A common FAQ is: "If this works, why has my doctor never mentioned it?"

Most doctors work within set routines and time limits, focusing on medication and acute issues—not on nervous system education or self-regulation practices, which aren't yet standard training. That doesn't mean the science is lacking.

Research indicates that stimulating the vagus nerve can help regulate factors such as inflammation, mood, and stress. A growing number of clinicians, particularly in integrative and trauma-informed care, are beginning to incorporate these techniques; however, change in medical practice is slow.

Another misconception is that you need costly gadgets or devices to stimulate the vagus nerve. While you might see wearable monitors or stimulators advertised, most of the best techniques—such as deep breathing, humming, gentle movement, or cold exposure—are free and accessible to everyone. Technology is optional, not essential.

Some people dismiss vagus nerve work as too complicated or "woo-woo," or believe only those experienced in meditation or yoga can benefit from it. In reality, these exercises are practical and straightforward, requiring no prior knowledge of mindfulness or neuroscience. You can start anytime—if you can breathe, hum, or splash cool water on your face, you already have what you need.

A big question is whether these practices can help with severe anxiety, trauma, or chronic illness. The reality is that vagus nerve exercises are not miracle cures.

They won't erase trauma, replace therapy, or instantly stop panic attacks. But they can help manage daily symptoms and improve resilience. For example, one reader, Julie, who had been skeptical after years of failed treatments, found that breathwork and vocal exercises reduced her panic attacks and improved her digestion within a few weeks. Such incremental progress is standard.

Many people worry about safety, especially if they have chronic illnesses or take medication.

Most vagus nerve techniques are gentle and safe, with minimal physical demands and no interaction with medicines. However, if you have a condition such as a heart rhythm disorder or are uncertain, consult your healthcare provider first. Listen to your body and adjust techniques as needed.

Another myth: "Vagus nerve exercises are just yoga or meditation in disguise." While there's overlap, these techniques target specific signals along the vagus nerve to particular effects. They go beyond generic relaxation—they actively help your body return to a state of balance after stress.

So, what can you expect from these practices? They offer practical tools for self-regulation—ways to steady yourself when symptoms or stress flare up. While not quick fixes or miracle solutions, they provide a foundation for gradual improvement. Results may include gentler mornings, fewer digestive issues, or more profound sleep. Change is often subtle at first but accumulates over time with regular practice.

If you're still skeptical, that's natural. Caution demonstrates that you value evidence and results. Remember, everyone's path is different; your experience matters most. What's essential is having tools that truly support you.

With these myths addressed, you now have a clearer sense of what vagus nerve exercises can and can't do. The following tools are designed for real life and real bodies—not perfection. Whether you aim to reduce anxiety, promote calmer digestion, or feel more like yourself, these practices are accessible.

Now that you understand how the vagus nerve works, the next step is learning how to recognize when your nervous system is asking for help.

Chapter 2

Signs You Need a Nervous System Reset

How to Spot Vagus Nerve Imbalance: Key Physical and Emotional Clues

Sometimes life feels like a game of whack-a-mole—one day it's a pounding head; the next, it's your stomach turning somersaults. You may have spent years searching for answers, moving from doctor to specialist while trying to make sense of symptoms that never seem to connect.

It's common to feel like your body is sending mixed messages, or that your mind and gut are arguing in a language you can't quite translate. If you're reading this, you've probably wondered whether something deeper is tying these "random" complaints together.

The truth is that your body often leaves clues. When the vagus nerve isn't functioning well, signals can appear in different ways—sometimes loud, sometimes subtle. You may not notice the pattern right away, but once you learn what to look for, those clues begin to form a clearer map.

Physical symptoms are often the first clues. You might experience frequent headaches, migraines, or constant pressure behind your eyes. At times, your heart may race or skip beats, even when you're sitting still or dealing with a small stressor.

Digestive symptoms are another common signal. Sudden nausea, burning reflux after meals, or persistent constipation may all reflect a nervous system struggling to stay balanced.

Some people find themselves clearing their throats constantly, struggling with hoarseness, or even losing their voice when stress builds. A chronic sore throat that never quite heals is another indication that your body's communication system is malfunctioning.

Emotional changes often follow physical symptoms. You may feel emotionally flat, as if nothing truly moves you. Laughter might feel forced, or tears refuse to come, even when you know something should affect you.

Irritability can also increase. Small frustrations may trigger outsized reactions, or a quiet undercurrent of anger may linger throughout the day.

The inability to relax—to truly unwind and let your guard down—might start to feel like your default setting. Mental fog creeps in, too. You misplace words mid-sentence, forget why you walked into a room, or struggle to focus on simple tasks. Stress only thickens the fog, making it harder to think clearly or remember details.

The overlap between the body and mind can be confusing, but it is itself a significant clue. You may notice that anxiety gives you butterflies—or more like angry hornets—in your belly. Or maybe it goes the other way: a night of tossing and turning leads to an edgy mood that lasts all day. The body and emotions are always talking to each other through the vagus nerve; when it's off-balance, every part of you feels it.

Self-Reflection Checklist: Are These Clues Showing Up for You?

- Do you get frequent headaches or migraines that seem connected to stress or fatigue?
- Does your heart race, flutter, or skip beats during moments of tension—even if there's no real danger?
- Have you battled unexplained digestive issues like nausea, reflux after meals, constipation that lingers for days, or a constant uneasy stomach?
- Do you notice changes in your voice—maybe a scratchiness, chronic sore throat, or voice fatigue—that get worse with stress?
- Is it hard to feel emotions deeply? Do you feel numb or disconnected from what's happening around you?
- Are irritability and sudden bursts of anger showing up more often than before? Do you struggle to relax even in "safe" settings?
- Does forgetfulness or mental fog seem worse when life gets busy or overwhelming?
- Do you clench your jaw at night or wake up with sore teeth from grinding?
- After social interactions—even ones you used to enjoy—do you feel drained entirely instead of energized?

If several of these sound familiar, you're not alone, and these signals deserve attention. These are not random irregularities or personal failings; they are real signals from your nervous system asking for support. Take a moment to note which ones stand out for you. This awareness is the first step toward understanding what your body needs.

When the vagus nerve is struggling, the clues can show up in unexpected combinations—sometimes all at once, sometimes in cycles that come and go. You may have days where everything feels fine until one small stressor tips the scale and triggers a wave of symptoms. Noticing these patterns doesn't mean labeling yourself as broken; it means recognizing that your system is asking for a reset.

Anxiety, Panic, and the Vagus Nerve: Recognizing "Fight-or-Flight" Traps

If you've ever felt your heart racing and your mind spinning with worst-case scenarios, you know panic's impact.

Your pounding pulse, shallow breathing, clammy hands, and churning stomach signal that your vagus nerve has stepped back while your fight-or-flight system takes over. Everyday events—a sudden text, a car horn, a crowded store—can trigger a reaction, making your body feel as if it's facing real danger. Sweaty palms, dizziness, trouble catching your breath, or an urge to escape are all common responses.

When the vagus nerve isn't functioning well, your body can become stuck in a constant "alert" state. Our ancestors relied on brief episodes of the fight-or-flight response to react quickly and survive immediate threats.

But if it gets stuck "on," everything feels hazardous, and you might overreact to minor stresses—a loud noise, an unexpected email, or an angry voice. It can feel impossible to "come down" even after the stress passes: your heart keeps pounding, your thoughts spiral, sleep feels impossible, and it's difficult to relax.

Often, particular situations sound the alarm—public speaking makes your chest tighten, and walking into a crowded room sparks an urge to escape. These are not signs of weakness or overreaction but messages from an overworked nervous system. Your body isn't flawed; it's trying to keep you safe in a world it perceives as unpredictable.

Recognizing these patterns is about understanding, not blame. Anxiety and panic aren't character flaws—they're protective responses, even if they misfire. The more you recognize these warning signs, the sooner you can respond to them with compassion and support. When panic strikes—racing thoughts, tightness, or dizziness—it's your body's signal for support, not for criticism.

Trauma Triggers and Sensory Overload: Understanding Your Body's Alarms

There's a big difference between everyday stress and the sudden, overwhelming waves that appear when trauma is triggered. Trauma triggers often arrive without warning and without regard for logic or timing. Something as simple as a scent while folding laundry can suddenly send your heart pounding or pull you toward a buried memory.

Flashbacks don't always look like scenes from a movie. Sometimes they appear as brief images, a rush of emotions, or physical sensations that are hard to explain.

At other times, there are no clear images at all—just a strange sense of disconnection, as if the world has faded to grayscale. This shutdown response, sometimes called dissociation, is the nervous system pulling the emergency brake.

Every day stress tends to build gradually—a strict deadline, a disagreement, a mountain of chores. You might be tense or distracted, but your sense of self stays intact. Trauma triggers, on the other hand, hijack your safety in an instant. It's not just being nervous or upset; it's an overpowering sense of fear or numbness that comes out of nowhere. Some people start to shake or feel cold, others grow heavy and stuck. If you ever find yourself inexplicably "shutting down" mid-day, trauma triggers may be at play.

Sensory overload is another indication that your nervous system is struggling. While anyone can experience overload, it's especially common for those with trauma histories, ADHD, autism, or heightened sensitivity.

Crowded places, blaring lights, or the beeps at the grocery store can set your nerves on edge. Sudden noises might make you flinch, and strong smells—from perfume to cleaning products—can leave you dizzy or nauseous. Even touch can overwhelm you; a scratchy sweater tag or an unexpected hug could leave you jumpy for hours.

Everyday situations become battlegrounds. Grocery shopping can feel more like a chore than a convenience, and family gatherings filled with overlapping conversations and clattering dishes can leave you feeling drained or irritable. Sometimes, it's a song on the radio—the one linked to a tough time—that tightens your chest and makes your palms sweat. Medical visits, with their sterile smells and bright lights, can bring everything to a head, setting off alarms you can't silence at will.

You might feel these same responses at unexpected times. An unpredictable phone buzz may spike your anxiety, and footsteps in the next room might leave you uneasy, even when you logically know there's no threat. Sometimes, even scrolling through social media—with its flashing images and constant notifications—leaves your body tense and your mind buzzing.

It's easy to be hard on yourself for these responses, thinking you're "too sensitive" or "overreacting." But your body is just trying to keep you safe. When your vagus nerve senses overload or a familiar threat, it triggers an instinctive alarm, pulling you out of the moment or flooding your body with adrenaline. These aren't faults—they're your nervous system working hard to shield you from danger.

If these experiences sound familiar—if certain places, sounds, touches, or smells make you freeze, panic, or want to vanish—you're not alone.

You're not broken or exaggerating; your system has just learned to prioritize safety. It remembers what matters most: protection. Understanding this isn't just about putting names to symptoms—it's about recognizing your body's need to feel secure.

What helps is knowing that none of these points lead to weakness or failure. It's how survival wiring works, especially after too many shocks or prolonged uncertainty. For many, the vagus nerve remains on high alert after trauma, scanning for danger even when the threat is long gone. You didn't choose this—your body adapted to survive hard times. Now, with new awareness and tools, you can teach your system to let go, even as life remains unpredictable.

Begin by noticing what situations trigger you. The next time you're overwhelmed by noise, touch, or emotion, pause and remind yourself that your system is reacting the way it learned to survive, not work against you. That kind of shift in perspective can gently reshape how you navigate the world and pave the path to healing—one trigger at a time.

Digestive Distress, Inflammation, and Fatigue: When the Body Speaks

There's a particular frustration that comes when your stomach acts up for what feels like the hundredth time, yet every doctor's visit ends with the same line: "Your tests look normal." You may leave feeling unseen or even questioning your own experience.

The reality is that your gut often reflects what's happening in your nervous system, especially when the vagus nerve is out of sync. During stressful periods, digestion can become unpredictable. Meals that once felt easy may suddenly cause bloating, cramping, or waves of nausea that make you regret eating at all.

You may experience constipation that won't budge or sudden flares of acid reflux after a difficult day. For some people, symptoms of irritable bowel syndrome seem to appear out of nowhere and worsen with each spike in stress or emotional strain.

It isn't "all in your head." When the vagus nerve isn't sending steady signals, the digestive tract can lose its natural rhythm, slowing down or becoming overly sensitive even when medical tests look normal.

There's also a strong link between nervous system imbalance and inflammation that many people miss. Maybe you've noticed that joint pain, muscle aches, or even skin issues like eczema or hives flare up after an argument, a tight deadline, or an emotional setback.

That pattern isn't random. When your body senses ongoing stress and your vagus nerve can't keep things regulated, inflammation surges. Your immune system goes into overdrive, leaving you stiff, sore, or battling skin flare-ups that make you feel uncomfortable in your own body.

Autoimmune conditions can become unpredictable—those days when pain or fatigue takes over seem to arrive on the heels of anxiety or after sleepless nights spent tossing and turning. It's no accident—your body responds this way because it's wired to protect you.

And then there's the exhaustion—a bone-deep tiredness that sleep never seems to fix. You might lie awake for hours, watching the clock tick by while your mind races. Even on the rare night you finally sleep, you wake up feeling unrested. Many people call this state "wired but tired"—when your body feels drained, yet your nervous system won't let you fully relax.

Minor stressors—a disagreement with a friend, a busy morning with the kids, a loud noise in the middle of the night—can drain you so quickly that you crash before noon. Energy becomes a scarce resource, carefully rationed to make it through the day. Coffee and willpower only go so far. Without proper vagal tone guiding your internal systems back to baseline, rest isn't restorative, and recovery feels out of reach.

Listening to your body's whispers can make all the difference. Maybe you've noticed you get stomach pains after tense conversations or headaches when life feels out of control. Perhaps you catch more colds when you're emotionally overwhelmed than when everyone else is sick. Your body tries to warn you before things get worse, sending subtle hints—a twinge in your gut, a patch of itchy skin, or a heavy wave of tiredness that sweeps over you out of nowhere.

These symptoms are your body's way of asking for attention. If you notice digestive flare-ups after arguments or find yourself battling fatigue after stressful weeks, take that as your cue: your nervous system needs support.

So often, these signals are dismissed or minimized—maybe by others, maybe by yourself. But I want to tell you they matter.

When your gut churns after a heated meeting, when joint pain spikes after bad news, or when you catch yet another cold during a rough patch at work, your body isn't failing you—it's speaking up in the only language it knows. Every whisper is an invitation to respond with care before those whispers become shouts that force you to stop altogether. The sooner you notice these early signs, the easier it becomes to break the cycle—one small step at a time.

Sometimes, this awareness alone feels like a relief. You realize that exhaustion isn't laziness and that digestive trouble isn't just bad luck with food. It's all part of a bigger pattern—your nervous system is calling for a reset.

The next time fatigue settles in early or your stomach rebels without warning, pause and check for stress simmering under the surface. With practice and patience, learning to respond to these cues can help restore balance and bring your system back to steady ground.

Self-Assessment Toolkit: Symptom Trackers and Progress Journals

When your body feels stuck in a loop, and your mind spins with questions, even a simple tool can bring clarity. Tracking helps—not to judge yourself, but to gently check in with your own experience.

Imagine having a notebook where you jot down how your anxiety, digestion, sleep, pain, and mood shift from day to day. Maybe you set up columns or color-code your notes—whatever format feels approachable.

You might rate each symptom from 1 to 5 or scribble a few words about how you felt after waking up, after meals, or before bed. The purpose isn't to obsess over every change but to start noticing the patterns hiding beneath the noise.

A daily check-in prompt can be surprisingly powerful. Try asking yourself, "How regulated did I feel today?"

There's no need for fancy language; write down if things felt balanced, off-kilter, chaotic, or somewhere in between. Over time, these quick reflections create a picture that's more honest than memory alone.

Maybe you'll notice that sleepless nights follow tense phone calls or that gut flares peak on Mondays. You're not aiming for perfection—no one gets it right every day. The goal is to understand what your body is trying to tell you so you can respond with more kindness and less frustration.

As you continue this practice, let your symptom tracker serve as a tool for curiosity rather than a source of criticism.

Instead of thinking, "Why am I still so tired?" try shifting to, "I notice I'm more tired on days when I skip breakfast," or "My mood dips when I haven't seen a friend all week." This tweak in perspective opens the door to self-compassion. Remember, you're not collecting data for anyone else—these notes are just for you.

If you find yourself getting discouraged by what you see, pause and remind yourself that noticing is a form of progress. You're learning to listen in a way most people never do.

Progress journaling adds another layer—a way to celebrate small victories you might otherwise overlook.

Maybe you write down moments like, "Recovered faster after a stressful work call," or, "Went out with friends and didn't feel wiped out after." It's easy to ignore these wins when symptoms are loud, but looking back at your journal can show you the slow build of resilience over time.

If sleep comes easier just once this week, that's worth recording. If you notice your gut is calm after using a breathing exercise, jot it down. These little milestones are signs that your nervous system is learning new rhythms.

Don't worry about making every entry perfect or filling out every column. The point is to show up honestly and with patience.

If it helps, pick out a special notebook or print out templates that feel inviting. Perhaps you use stickers or doodles on both tough and good days—whatever enables you to stay engaged.

Once a week, take a few minutes to revisit your notes. Look for even the tiniest shifts: fewer headaches, more energy in the mornings, and a sense of calm after trying a new exercise. These reflections aren't just records—they're encouragement that change is happening, even when it's slow.

Please keep these journals handy as we progress through the following chapters together. The insights you gather will help tailor routines to fit your specific ups and downs. You'll also have tangible proof of progress when doubt creeps in or motivation dips. Over time, you'll turn these pages into a conversation with yourself—a space where you meet both setbacks and successes with curiosity, not judgment.

As this chapter comes to a close, remember that awareness is your first step toward finding balance and relief. Patterns, once hidden in the chaos, will soon become visible markers on your roadmap to wellness. With each note and reflection, you're building a foundation for real change—one that goes deeper than symptoms alone. Next, we'll lay out the groundwork for safe and inclusive healing practices that meet you where you are, regardless of the complexity of your life.

Chapter 3

Foundations of Safe and Inclusive Healing

Creating Your Safe Space: Preparing for Nervous System Work

Think about the last time you truly felt at ease. It could be a cozy Sunday morning, wrapped in your favorite blanket, sunlight softening the edges of your room. Or perhaps it's been so long since you felt safe that the idea itself seems almost foreign, like a language you once spoke but have forgotten.

If you're living with anxiety, chronic illness, or the aftershocks of trauma, "relaxing" can sound like a cruel joke.

The truth is that your nervous system needs signals of safety before it can accept healing. Creating a safe space—whether physical or imagined—isn't just some fluffy ritual; it's the groundwork for real change.

Start with what you can touch and see. If possible, choose a spot in your home that feels quiet and undisturbed—even if it's just a favorite chair or a small corner by a window. If silence isn't possible, try to reduce sudden noises by closing a door, putting your phone on silent, or using a white noise machine.

Adjust the lighting so it feels gentle on your senses. Harsh overhead bulbs can keep the nervous system on edge, so consider using a warm lamp or candle instead. Even small changes in lighting can influence how quickly the body begins to settle.

If you enjoy soft scents, add a drop of lavender or chamomile oil to a tissue or diffuser. Familiar aromas can signal to your brain that this is a moment for comfort rather than vigilance. Weighted blankets or plush throws can also provide a gentle pressure that many people find grounding.

The goal isn't perfection—it's intention. Notice what helps you feel sheltered and at ease, even if it's only for a few minutes.

Sensory cues can also support this process. Choose sounds that calm rather than distract, such as soft music or nature sounds like rainfall, ocean waves, or birdsong. There's no single right option—let your ears guide you.

You might also surround yourself with objects that represent safety or belonging. A photograph of someone who makes you smile, a smooth stone you enjoy holding, or a mug from a favorite trip can quietly reinforce a sense of comfort.

Soft fabrics can make a difference, too. Loose cotton clothing or warm socks may seem like small details, but they can help your body relax when your senses feel sensitive. Each choice you make adds another layer to the environment you are creating.

Before you begin any nervous system practice, consider starting with a ritual that gently signals to your body that this space and time are for healing.

A simple stretch—such as rolling your neck or shrugging your shoulders—can help release tension and bring you into the present moment. Placing a hand over your heart or resting both hands on your belly can be grounding, letting you feel warmth and rhythm beneath your skin.

If sipping a cup of warm tea soothes you, let yourself enjoy those first few sips in silence. These little cues are like opening acts before the main event; they tell your body it's finally okay to relax its guard.

Of course, not everyone has control over their environment. Maybe your home is noisy, crowded, or doesn't feel like your own. That doesn't mean you can't build safety into your practice—you absolutely can.

Portable safe spaces live in your imagination and senses. Guided imagery exercises can be helpful—close your eyes and picture a place where you feel peace or freedom, whether real or imagined. Imagine the colors, textures, smells, and sounds as vividly as possible.

If visualization feels tough, anchor yourself with affirmations: quietly repeating, "I am safe at this moment," even if only half-believed at first, can nudge your nervous system toward calm. Noise-canceling headphones or an eye mask can block out the world just enough to create a bubble of privacy.

Reflection Prompt: Designing Your Sanctuary

Pick up a notebook and write your answers to the following questions—no need for perfect wording, just honest reflection:

- What colors, textures, or objects help me feel most comfortable?
- Is there a specific music or sound that instantly makes me breathe

easier?

- Are there scents—herbal tea, spices, fresh air—that bring back good memories?
- What small rituals help me mark "this is my time" (lighting a candle, stretching, holding a photo)?
- If I can't control my space right now, what images or affirmations help me feel grounded?

Use this list as inspiration when preparing for practice. Over time, you'll discover which details matter most for creating safety—not just for vagus nerve work but for any moment life feels too much.

Creating safety is not about chasing perfection; it's about giving yourself permission to slow down and care for every part of you that still carries caution or fatigue. Even tiny changes—a softer lightbulb, a favorite song—can be enough to shift your body from alert to receptive.

Trauma-Informed Practice: Gentle Approaches for Sensitive Nervous Systems

Working with your nervous system can sometimes surface unexpected emotions, especially if there's a trauma history. Even gentle exercises may trigger overwhelming memories or make relaxation feel unsafe. If relaxing makes you uneasy, know you're not alone—this is your protective system at work, not a personal failing. Many people with trauma backgrounds react this way; it's a profoundly human response.

Choice and control are essential in the healing process. Every exercise here is an invitation, not a command. You're always in charge—pause, skip, or adapt anything that doesn't feel right. Trust your intuition; go at your own pace. If something feels too overwhelming, consider a smaller or gentler practice. Healing is not a race.

Modify practices to feel safer. If closing your eyes feels uncomfortable during an exercise, keep them open. When firm emotions surface, try holding a grounding object—such as a stone or a fidget toy—to help you feel more centered. If lying down feels too exposed, sit or stand by a wall for support. There's no wrong way to care for yourself—adapt as needed.

Trauma responses may emerge during practice: you may experience dissociation, shaking, unexpected crying, or feel the urge to leave. These reactions are not failures—just your body's old protective patterns. If overwhelmed, ground yourself: name five things you see, touch something solid, or repeat, "I am safe right now." It's okay to stop and self-soothe whenever you need to.

Modifications for Limited Mobility, Chronic Pain, and Fatigue

Everybody is different. Yours might carry the scars of old injuries, the heaviness of pain, or the fatigue that never seems to let up. You may experience stiffness, unpredictable energy, or physical limitations that fluctuate from day to day. If you've ever glanced at a list of wellness exercises and thought, "That looks impossible for me," you're not alone.

Too often, books and guides overlook individuals whose bodies function differently. Vagus nerve practices welcome everyone—you don't need to be flexible, pain-free, or energetic to begin. Your body, precisely as it is, can benefit from these tools—even if that means making adjustments.

Chronic illness, disability, or pain does not disqualify anyone from this work. You spend much of your day in a chair or bed. You may have a diagnosis that makes movement unpredictable. None of that shuts you out—you still belong here.

On the contrary, your nervous system may need even more gentle support. Sometimes, just reading about movement can trigger frustration or sadness because you remember what your body could once do—or because even small actions now cost so much. Take a breath and honor that feeling. It is real. At the same time, I want you to feel invited into these practices, not pushed out.

Let's start by discussing the adaptation of breathwork.

If lying flat is uncomfortable or makes breathing more difficult, try sitting upright with your feet on the floor. Place a pillow behind your lower back or under your knees for extra support. If sitting is tiring, recline with cushions propped behind you. The point isn't about achieving perfect posture; it's about finding ease so your breath can move freely without restriction.

For those with respiratory challenges, take shorter breaths and rest as needed. Even one slow inhale and exhale counts—there's no minimum requirement here.

Moving on to gentle movement and self-massage, you don't have to stand, twist, or stretch beyond your limits to activate your vagus nerve.

Chair-based neck rolls or gentle tilts can be just as effective as more traditional stretches. Use a hand to softly massage your jawline or the back of your neck while sitting comfortably. If your hands tire quickly, try using a softball or massage tool instead of direct pressure. On some days, you may only feel up to moving your fingers or turning your head slightly; those small actions are enough.

Pillows and supports are not just comforts—they're tools for accessibility. Suppose you want to try a movement practice but feel wobbly or sore; place pillows beside your hips, behind your back, or under your arms for extra stability. Rolled towels make great supports for knees or ankles. Leaning against a wall during standing exercises can reduce the fear of falling and make the experience safer.

Reducing exertion is crucial if fatigue stalks you or pain flares easily. There's no need to push through discomfort or chase significant results in a single session.

Practice just one exercise at a time—maybe two gentle repetitions instead of ten. Allow yourself longer rest periods between movements; sometimes, taking five slow breaths between each action is what keeps things sustainable. If your energy is running low, pause and check in with yourself—do you need water, a break, or to take a break altogether? Listening to your body is not a sign of "failing" at healing; it's a wise act of self-preservation.

Self-advocacy matters most when learning what works for your unique situation. Keep a small journal handy and jot down notes after practice: How much energy did you have before? Did pain increase or decrease? Was there a movement or position that offered relief? Tracking these details over time helps you notice patterns—maybe certain days of the week are better for practice, or perhaps mornings are easier than evenings.

It can help to create a "modification menu." List the different ways you might adjust an exercise to match how you feel on any given day—seated instead of standing, shorter sessions instead of longer ones, using props, or skipping them altogether. On difficult days when motivation dips or symptoms flare, having this menu ready removes the mental burden of having to figure everything out from scratch.

Healing is not about hitting milestones set by someone else—it's about honoring where you are and making choices that serve you in this moment. Some days will be slow and gentle; others may surprise you with more energy or range of motion than expected. Either way, every effort—no matter how small—signals to your nervous system that relief is possible and that it deserves care.

Recognizing and Responding to Triggers During Practice

While practicing vagus nerve exercises, it's normal for strong emotions or physical sensations to bubble up. You might notice your breath racing, thoughts spinning out of control, or tension locking into your jaw and shoulders. Sometimes, your heart thumps harder, or you get the sudden urge to move, stop what you're doing, or even leave the room altogether.

These are not signs that you're failing or that something is wrong with you. Instead, they're clues—clear signals from your nervous system that it feels threatened or on high alert. Think of them like the dashboard lights in your car. They don't mean you should quit; they let you know that some part of you still feels unsafe.

Spotting these early signs makes all the difference. If your chest tightens or your breathing speeds up, take a moment to pause and breathe deeply. Notice whether your muscles clench, your stomach churns, or your hands grow cold. Even a wave of restlessness or a strong need to look around the room can be your body's way of scanning for safety.

Some people feel like they're dissociating or "floating away," while others become hyperaware of tiny sounds or sensations. It might even be a subtle shift—a slight shiver, a prickly sensation on your skin, or a heaviness behind your eyes. The sooner you catch these cues, the sooner you can respond with care.

Responding to these triggers with compassion is vital. You don't need to battle your body's alarms; in fact, gentle self-talk works far better than criticism.

When anxiety, panic, or fear shows up, try telling yourself, "This is just my body protecting me." It sounds simple, but these words can help soften self-judgment and create space for kindness. If you feel the urge to stop an exercise, honor that instinct. There's no badge for powering through distress—pausing is wisdom, not weakness. Turn your attention to your breath and see if you can lengthen each exhale just a bit. Slow exhalations signal safety to your nervous system, helping it settle without force or control.

Sometimes, triggers build up until you feel stuck or overwhelmed. Having a menu of reset techniques offers a way back to safety when things get rough.

Splashing cool water on your face, even if it's just a few drops around your temples or neck, can help jolt your system out of panic and into the present. Some people keep a small stone, bead, or fidget toy nearby—something to squeeze or roll between your fingers. This physical anchor draws your focus back to what's real and steady.

You might also find comfort in grounding statements, spoken softly or even silently: "I am here," "I am safe," or "This will pass." Pairing these words with deep breaths adds another layer of reassurance.

When visual cues help more than words, close your eyes (if that feels okay) and picture someone who makes you feel safe—a friend, a pet, or even a favorite teacher from childhood.

Imagine their presence beside you as you breathe. Alternatively, picture a place where you've always felt at peace: under a tree, near the ocean, curled up on a sunlit couch. Let those details—colors, sounds, textures—fill your mind until your heartbeat steadies and your breath slows down.

It's essential to recognize when additional support is required. If distress keeps building or doesn't fade after practicing reset techniques, reach out to someone trustworthy—a therapist, a counselor, or a close friend who understands what you're facing.

Persistent flashbacks, panic attacks that don't resolve with grounding, or feelings of being trapped in old memories are signals that professional help could be valuable. There's no shame in needing backup; sometimes, healing requires the support of another voice or hand.

The reality is that triggers are part of this work for many people. You may find yourself cycling through calm and activation more than once in a single session. That's okay.

Notice the patterns: Does a specific exercise always evoke fear? Does fatigue set in after particular movements? These observations are information—not judgments—guiding you toward what works best for you right now.

If journaling helps you process what happens during practice, jot down notes after each session. Record what triggered discomfort and which reset strategies worked (or didn't). Over time, these notes will reveal trends and offer reassurance on hard days—proof that progress isn't about perfection but about learning what helps you feel safe and steady in your skin.

Triggers may appear from time to time. The difference comes from how gently and quickly you meet them—with understanding instead of blame, with tools that bring relief instead of shame. Each compassionate response helps retrain both mind and body to trust that it's possible to move through discomfort without being consumed by it.

Building a Resilience Toolkit: Grounding and Self-Compassion Habits

A resilience toolkit is your collection of strategies—practices, rituals, and comforts—that help you regain balance during tough times. Think of it as a mental backpack filled with things that bring you back to the center when anxiety, pain, or past stressors arise. This toolkit grows with you; as you discover what works, you'll add new tools, let go of others, and stumble upon surprising comforts along the way.

Grounding techniques form the core of this kit. They're simple, adaptable, and effective. Some people find slow, deep breathing—especially extending the exhale—calms their body. Others rely on sensory input, such as the scent of peppermint oil, the coolness of a smooth stone, or the pressure of a softball.

You can release tension by using gentle movements, like walking around the room or swaying in place. There's no single "right" method—the goal is to reconnect with your body and the present moment.

Self-compassion is just as vital for nervous system healing. Frustration is natural when panic returns or fatigue complicates things. In those moments, your toolkit should include a kind inner voice: "I'm doing my best, and that's enough."

These aren't empty words; studies show that self-compassion reduces stress hormones and inflammation. When setbacks occur, responding to yourself with kindness helps you bounce back rather than descending into self-criticism. Affirmations can be simple: "I am worthy of care" or "It's okay to rest." Even quietly thinking or whispering these phrases helps shift your nervous system away from stress.

Practical exercises are essential. Sensory grounding remains popular because it's fast and works nearly anywhere. Try the "5-4-3-2-1" technique: notice five things you see, four you can touch, three you hear, two you smell, and one you taste. This sequence halts racing thoughts and centers you in the now.

Gentle self-massage—such as circling your palm, stroking your jaw, or pressing your fingertips to your temples—sends calming signals to your brain. Mantras or calming phrases, such as "Peace begins with me," repeated with each breath, help lay down neural pathways of calm.

As you read this book, start a journal page dedicated to your resilience toolkit. Record each grounding technique you try, noting what felt good, what felt odd, and when it helped most. Over time, your journal will become a reference, reminding you which tools to use when stress clouds your memory. Be open to experimenting. Running cool water over your wrists works best, or listening to rain sounds helps you relax immediately. The more options you collect, the more empowered you'll feel to handle challenges.

Remember, your toolkit should evolve in tandem with your needs and experiences. Jot down new ideas as you encounter them—perhaps you'll find humming intriguing or want to try cold exposure on a tough day. Let inspiration from friends, readings, or unexpected moments of peace guide you. Include these discoveries in your journal; each small addition increases your resilience.

A well-rounded resilience toolkit enables you to face challenges resourcefully rather than reactively. It reminds your body that discomfort isn't a threat and that relief is always within reach, even if it's just one breath away. Your personalized collection of grounding habits and self-compassionate phrases will become a safety net, supporting you before panic or exhaustion sets in.

Healing the nervous system is a gradual process—it takes time to identify practices that suit your unique needs and feel natural in your body. The following section will explore daily routines and how tiny rituals fit into everyday life, making healing habits as instinctive as breathing or stretching after a long day. With every tool you add, you move closer to deep, lasting calm—and that's worth celebrating.

Chapter 4

The Science of Vagus Nerve Activation (Without the Jargon)

How Vagus Nerve Stimulation Calms Anxiety and Panic Attacks

Imagine you're stuck in traffic, running late, while anxiety floods your body—your heart pounds, breathing quickens, palms sweat. Your body has triggered its ancient alarm system—the fight-or-flight response—despite the everyday stressor. The good news: you have an internal switch to quiet this alarm—the vagus nerve. Learning to activate this "switch" lets you quickly dial down anxiety.

Starting at the base of the brain, the vagus nerve travels through the neck, chest, and abdomen, helping regulate essential functions such as steady breathing, a calm heart rate, and the relaxation of internal organs.

Stress triggers adrenaline, launching you into fight-or-flight mode, but stimulating the vagus nerve sends calming signals that slow your heartbeat and deepen your breath. Techniques like slow breathing or humming feel almost magical in their effects, but it's just biology in action.

Vagus nerve activation works by directly countering adrenaline and communicating with your heart to slow and steady its rhythm. It promotes long, deep exhales that send "safety" signals to your brain. These signals help turn down the body's stress response, soften muscle tension, and restore calm, much like lowering the stress "volume" so your mind and body can reset.

This idea may sound simple, but it is supported by scientific research. For instance, slow diaphragmatic breathing—with deeper, longer exhales—has been shown to lower anxiety almost immediately.

Clinical trials have demonstrated that such practices reduce heart rate, stabilize cardiac rhythms, and increase feelings of calm, more so than doing nothing. Studies also show that non-invasive vagus nerve stimulation devices—gadgets placed on the ear or neck—help reduce anxiety and panic. Whether it is equipment or simple breathwork, these methods reliably activate the vagus nerve.

Why do things like humming or slow exhaling work so fast during panic? Humming vibrates the throat and chest, directly stimulating the vagus nerve, like a gentle cue to your nervous system to relax.

This physical signal interrupts spiraling thoughts and anchors you in the present. Likewise, long exhalations send strong "relax" messages via the vagus nerve, calming the body and mind. Singers and wind musicians often feel at peace after practice because their parasympathetic, or "rest-and-digest," system switches on.

A reader avoided a panic attack on a subway by humming quietly to herself when she felt the familiar chest tightness. The sensation of humming distracted her from fear, and within minutes, her heart rate slowed, and anxiety faded, allowing her to finish her commute without incident.

Try It Now: The Two-Minute Vagus Reset

1. Sit comfortably and place a hand on your chest or belly.
2. Take a slow breath in through your nose as you count to four.
3. Slowly breathe out through pursed lips, extending the exhale to a count of six or eight.
4. Add a soft hum on each exhale, feeling the vibrations.
5. Repeat for one to two minutes.

You may experience warmth or a sense of release. Even subtle relief grows with practice, and soon, this reset can become your go-to technique for calming anxiety anywhere.

Armed with these simple, science-backed tools, you finally have real ways to flip your internal "calm" switch and manage stress as it arises.

Rewiring Trauma Responses: The Vagus Nerve's Role in Emotional Healing

Living with trauma often means having a hypersensitive nervous system, always on edge, even when no real threat is present. After trauma, the body's "danger alarm" is recalibrated to perceive non-threatening cues as dangerous, causing hypervigilance, muscle tension, and fatigue. Simple assurance rarely helps because these reactions are rooted in the body's learned response to fear. The vagus nerve, however, provides a pathway to retrain the nervous system for safety.

Through gentle daily exercises, you can help your body pause before reacting, gradually teaching your "faulty alarm" not to overreact. This process increases heart rate variability (HRV), a measure of the nervous system's ability to adapt to environmental changes. Higher HRV enables smoother transitions between alert and rest states, reducing startle responses and tension.

This transformation relies on neuroplasticity—your brain's ability to form new, healthier pathways. Regular vagus nerve exercises reinforce these changes, making it easier to access calm states and weakening the automatic panic response.

For example, Tasha tracked her trauma symptoms in a journal while practicing daily humming and breathwork. Over eight weeks, she noticed reduced panic during triggers, increased moments of presence, and fewer flashbacks. Her body began to trust that not every discomfort signaled danger, even though her trauma remained.

Taming Inflammation and Autoimmunity: Science-Backed Benefits

If you struggle with chronic pain, swollen joints, rashes, or unpredictable gut issues, it can sometimes feel like your body is constantly working against itself.

In many people, the immune system contributes to a persistent "silent fire" of inflammation—not only from injuries or infections but also in conditions such as rheumatoid arthritis, Crohn's disease, lupus, or IBS.

In this process, the vagus nerve helps regulate the body's response. It helps the brain and immune system stay in contact, influencing how inflammation rises or settles in the body.

Research suggests that healthy vagal tone can help calm excessive inflammatory signaling, supporting the body's natural ability to maintain balance.

This mechanism is well-established in biology: the vagus nerve can "flip the switch" on inflammation, signaling to your body that it's safe to focus on repair rather than defense. However, chronic stress can weaken or overload the vagus nerve, leaving the immune system stuck in an "attack" mode even when there's no real threat. Over time, this leads to persistent symptoms, such as aching, swollen joints, gut flares after stressful events, rashes that worsen with overwhelm, and headaches triggered by emotional stress.

Studies support these observations. In rheumatoid arthritis, stimulating the vagus nerve—through gentle electrical pulses or breathing exercises—has been shown to reduce markers of inflammation and improve symptoms.

Similarly, Crohn's disease patients who received vagus nerve stimulation experienced fewer flare-ups and required less medication. A decade of research has shown a clear trend: stronger vagal tone (a sign of a healthy vagus nerve) is associated with less pain, swelling, and fewer autoimmune attacks.

Importantly, you don't need special machines or a clinical setting to harness these benefits. Every day routines can have powerful effects. Chronic stress lowers vagal tone, allowing inflammation to worsen. In contrast, regular vagus nerve exercises—like humming, slow breathing, or gentle neck stretches—help reduce inflammation by signaling to your system that it's safe to heal.

Take Miguel, a 42-year-old accountant who struggled with IBS and autoimmune joint pain for years. Stressful events triggered his gut cramps and joint swelling; medications helped, but didn't break the cycle.

Once Miguel began adding vagus nerve exercises to his mornings and evenings—breathing before breakfast, humming during commutes, gentle neck rolls at his desk—he experienced fewer digestive flares and less joint swelling after stressful days. The symptoms didn't disappear, but Miguel gained more control. He learned to anticipate and manage flare-ups, which reduced their intensity.

What's happening inside Miguel's body—and possibly yours—is rooted in real science. Activating your vagus nerve through simple daily habits helps regulate immune activity and prevent inflammation from spiraling out of control. Your nervous system learns new rhythms: stress doesn't automatically mean pain or swelling, because your body's internal peacekeeper is finally active again. Over time, those wild symptom swings settle; your baseline becomes more stable.

If you keep a journal or symptom tracker, you may notice patterns: perhaps meetings used to trigger gut symptoms, but with slow breathing beforehand, they don't. Humming in the evening can help relieve joint pain that often follows family gatherings. These small daily actions add up, resulting in less inflammation, greater comfort, and a sense of control over your health.

In short, your vagus nerve stands at the crossroads of immunity, inflammation, stress, and healing. Each breath, hum, stretch, or mindful pause is a way to calm your immune system and foster healing from the inside out.

Improving Digestion and Gut Health Through Vagus Nerve Regulation

Digestive struggles can feel relentless. Maybe your stomach twists after lunch, or you find yourself bloated for hours following a stressful day.

Many people don't realize that the vagus nerve acts as the principal conductor of your digestive orchestra. As soon as you see or smell food, your brain activates the vagus nerve, preparing your stomach to release digestive acids and enzymes.

Once you start eating, this same nerve keeps everything moving forward—literally—by coordinating peristalsis. These gentle wave-like contractions push food along your intestines. Every step of digestion relies on healthy vagal communication—from breaking down the first bite to absorbing nutrients and eliminating waste.

When the vagus nerve is active and regulated, it signals your digestive tract to work smoothly. Stomach acid rises to help break down proteins. The pancreas releases digestive enzymes, while the gallbladder delivers bile that helps break down fats. Peristalsis keeps things flowing, so food doesn't sit too long and cause discomfort or fermentation.

If this nerve goes "offline" under stress, however, the whole process grinds to a halt. You might feel your stomach clench, experience cramps, or even sudden diarrhea, or notice that food sits heavy and slowly. Chronic constipation, erratic bowel habits, or unpredictable bloating can all point back to a frazzled vagus nerve.

Several studies suggest that vagus nerve exercises support better gut health. Studies have shown that slow breathing and gentle humming before meals can increase vagal tone, helping digestion move more efficiently and easing symptoms of irritable bowel syndrome (IBS), constipation, and bloating.

These practices help "wake up" the nerve, restoring its ability to communicate clearly with your gut.

Other studies have tracked gut-brain signaling by observing how stress disrupts this pathway. They found that regular vagus nerve activation may help restore this communication, leading to more consistent digestion and fewer flare-ups.

Stress and digestion feed off each other in a vicious loop. Stress tightens the body and signals the digestive tract to slow or even stop. That's why arguments at dinner or rushing through meals often lead to stomach pain or heartburn. Your body can't focus on digestion when it still feels threatened.

If you've ever noticed more symptoms during high-pressure weeks, you're not imagining things. The vagus nerve sits at this crossroads: when you find ways to relax before eating—like taking a few slow breaths or humming quietly—you send a direct "all clear" down the line to your gut. That signal helps your body shift from survival mode to "rest-and-digest," making it easier to absorb nutrients and avoid those painful after-meal episodes.

Sarah's experience is an excellent illustration of this feedback loop in real life. For months, she dreaded dinner because bloating and cramps always followed.

After learning about vagus nerve regulation, she decided to pause before each meal and take five deep, slow breaths while rubbing her hands together for warmth. This simple routine helped turn off her body's stress alarms. Within two weeks, her post-meal bloating decreased dramatically, and she felt more comfortable in her skin after eating.

To make this process more transparent, imagine tracing a meal through your digestive system with the vagus nerve guiding each step:

1. **See or smell food:** The brain fires signals, and the vagus nerve tells the stomach to get ready by releasing acid.

2. **Chew and swallow:** The Vagus nerve stimulates the saliva and swallowing reflex.

3. **Food enters the stomach, where acid** and enzymes break it down, and peristalsis moves it onward through the digestive tract.

4. **Into the small intestine:** Your body releases enzymes and bile. Nutrients are absorbed.

5. **Large intestine:** Vagus nerve supports peristalsis for smooth transit → Waste is eliminated.

When stress takes over, and the vagus nerve is "offline," these steps break down: stomach acid production decreases, peristalsis slows or stops, enzyme release is impaired, and digestion becomes stuck or chaotic. You might feel heavy, nauseated, or develop trapped gas because the signals never reach their destination.

Visual: Tracing a Meal with Your Vagus Nerve

- Brain (see/smell food) → Stomach ("get ready!")
- Chew/swallow → Esophagus (saliva/relaxation)
- Stomach → Small intestine (digest/absorb)
- Small intestine → Large intestine (move/clear out)
- Large intestine → Brain ("all done!")

These arrows flow freely when calm prevails, but get blocked by stress-induced static when the vagus nerve can't do its job.

Building in daily vagal exercises—especially before meals—helps keep these signals clear and steady. Whether it's slow breathing at the table, humming as you cook, or gentle neck stretches before breakfast, these small routines can noticeably improve your digestion and overall comfort. The more you support your vagus nerve, the more reliable your gut becomes—and the less often you're caught off guard by pain or discomfort after eating.

Sleep, Fatigue, and HRV: The Vagus Nerve's Impact on Restorative Sleep

Falling asleep shouldn't feel like climbing a mountain every night. For many people, though, drifting into deep rest can seem impossible. Racing thoughts, a restless body, or waking up feeling drained are everyday struggles.

One reason for this hidden exhaustion is the way your nervous system shifts between "on" and "off" states. The vagus nerve helps shift the body out of daytime alertness and into the calmer state where real sleep begins.

When the vagus nerve activates, it signals the parasympathetic system—your internal "sleep mode"—to take over. Muscles release tension, breathing slows, and the mind begins to settle. What follows isn't just relaxation; it's the body responding to a biological cue to repair and recharge.

Science is showing that supporting the vagus nerve may improve sleep quality and energy levels. Investigations have found that when people practice simple stimulation techniques—such as specific breathing patterns or gentle vocalizations—sleep difficulties often improve.

Evidence indicates that stimulating the vagus nerve before bedtime may help people fall asleep more easily and experience deeper rest. In observations involving individuals with chronic fatigue or persistent sleep problems, some participants reported fewer nighttime awakenings and more refreshing mornings after incorporating nightly vagal exercises.

One reason may be that vagus nerve activation increases heart rate variability (HRV), an important marker of nervous system flexibility and recovery.

Heart rate variability might sound technical, but it's pretty simple. Imagine your heartbeat as a drummer—sometimes fast, sometimes slow, constantly adjusting to the rhythm of life. When HRV is high, your body can shift easily between action and rest. When it's low, you may feel stuck in one mode or constantly tired. HRV serves as a report card for resilience.

High HRV usually means your body handles stress more effectively, recovers from difficult days, and recharges during sleep. Low HRV often shows up as chronic fatigue, ongoing sleep issues, or the feeling of being "wired but tired."

You don't need fancy gadgets to notice changes. Still, if you're curious, wearable devices and phone apps can provide numbers you can track over time. What matters most is how you feel: do you wake up refreshed or still dragging? Can you recover from a stressful week, or does it take a long time to feel normal again?

Stories from real people can make these changes easier to understand. Dylan used to dread bedtime—he would toss and turn for hours, counting down until sunrise with heavy eyes and a foggy mind.

After adding five minutes of slow breathing and gentle humming before bed each night, he began to fall asleep more quickly. Within a few weeks, his mornings felt different—he actually wanted to get out of bed. His family even noticed that he seemed calmer and more present during breakfast.

Another reader described using a short routine—breathing in for four counts and out for seven while lying down with one hand on her heart. Over time, she found that she could sleep through the night without waking up gasping or anxious.

Minor adjustments to nighttime habits can be surprisingly effective. Building a simple pre-sleep routine—maybe three minutes of slow breathing or humming quietly—tells your body it's safe to shift gears. You create a new association: "This is my time to settle down." Over days and weeks, your vagus nerve gets better at flipping the switch from alert to restful, making deep sleep more likely.

Fatigue isn't just about not sleeping enough; it's about not getting quality rest when you do sleep. Vagus nerve routines help restore the natural ebb and flow between wakefulness and recovery. With practice, you'll find it easier to let go of tension at night—and finally wake up with energy to meet the day.

As you reach the end of this chapter, remember—your nervous system naturally cycles between activity and rest. Supporting your vagus nerve builds the foundation for proper recovery, not just at night but throughout your daily life. The next chapter will guide you through routines and exercises tailored for everyday use, allowing you to incorporate these science-backed habits into your bedtime routine and beyond.

Chapter 5

Rapid-Access Calm: Core Vagus Nerve Exercises for Everyday Stress

"2-Minute Reset" Breathing for Instant Calm

Stress can strike unexpectedly—your chest tightens before a tough conversation, or your thoughts race after a poor night's sleep. The need to escape, freeze, or react can feel overwhelming, as if your body is stuck on high alert.

If you've ever wished for a "pause button" before panic or tension takes over, this "2-Minute Reset" breathing technique gives you exactly that. No silence, no special setup, and no complicated skills—just your breath and two minutes.

The core of this practice is the "elongated exhale" method, which helps shift your body out of fight-or-flight mode and into a state of calm.

Here's how: get comfortable in any position—sitting, standing, even lying down. Place a hand over your belly or chest to focus your attention and help you connect with your breath.

Take a slow breath in through your nose to a count of four, letting your belly gently expand. Then, exhale gently through pursed lips or with a soft "shhh" sound for a count of eight. The exhale should last longer than the inhale—this is key. Repeat for two minutes, or as long as you need, until your body feels at ease.

What's happening during this exercise? The long exhale directly signals your vagus nerve, telling your body it's okay to relax.

As the central highway between your brain and organs, especially the heart and lungs, the vagus nerve responds to slow outbreaths by promoting relaxation. Heart rate slows, muscles unclench, and blood pressure drops. Studies confirm that prolonged exhaling increases parasympathetic (rest-and-digest) activity, thereby rapidly easing both the body and the mind. It's like flipping a switch from chaos to clarity.

If you're new to breathwork, or if focusing on your breath makes you dizzy or anxious—especially if you have trauma or panic history—know that's normal.

For these moments, anchoring with a hand on your chest or belly helps ground you in the present. If counting your breath feels stressful, inhale deeply and let the exhale be comfortably long—no numbers needed. Another helpful tactic is to purse your lips, as if gently blowing out a candle, or use a soft "shhh" sound on the exhale. These provide sensory feedback to focus your mind.

Breathing exercises aren't one-size-fits-all. If you have asthma, COPD, or other breathing conditions, be gentle—never force deep breathing. Try shorter cycles, such as three seconds in and five seconds out. Suppose nasal breathing isn't possible (due to congestion or allergy), breathe out through your mouth. In that case, the goal is comfort and ease, not technical perfection.

For those who prefer more structure, try "box breathing": inhale for four counts, hold for four, exhale for four, hold for four, and repeat. It adds balance and extra steadiness when you're anxious.

Life isn't always quiet or private. Stress often spikes in public or noisy places—such as on a bus, at work, or at home—making it difficult to focus. The beauty of this reset is its flexibility. Eyes can be open, and you can do it while walking, or even during a short bathroom break.. In moments of tension—before appointments, in arguments, or lying awake at night—even a single round can help. If you lose track or get interrupted, start again without self-judgment.

Interactive Element: Your Personal Reset Cheat Sheet

On a sticky note or any other piece of paper, write your favorite cue for reset breathing—like "hand on heart," "soft 'shhh' sound," or "4 in, 8 out." Place it somewhere visible, such as by your desk, in your wallet, or next to your bed. When stress rises, please take a moment to acknowledge it and do a round of reset breathing. Even one cycle helps remind your nervous system that you can access a calm state.

This practice may seem simple, but it is powerful, especially for those overwhelmed by anxiety, pain flares, digestive issues, or fatigue. With every slow exhale, you prove to yourself that relief isn't just possible—it's already within you.

Humming and Chanting: Vibrational Techniques for Down-Regulation

Humming is a simple, effective way to calm an overactive nervous system. When feeling anxious or tired, humming offers an easy shortcut to relief—no need for a quiet room or special skills, just a willingness to make sound.

To start, close your mouth, relax your lips, and breathe in through your nose. Hum softly as you exhale, noticing the vibration in your throat and chest. Focus on comfort, not volume. You can sit or recline, inhale, close your lips, and hum as you exhale. Repeat for several breaths, feeling the easing effect on your body.

The soothing effect of humming comes from vibration, which activates the vagus nerve. As your vocal folds vibrate, they send calming signals that move your body away from the stress response and into "rest and digest." Humming or chanting helps regulate the nervous system through sound-based practices.

Practices like chanting 'OM' in yoga work in a similar way—by combining breath and vibration to induce calm. Options include basic humming, OM chanting, singing a note, or vowel sounds like "mmm," "ooo," or "ahh." You can also try resonance breathing, making any soft, pleasant sound as you exhale.

Experiment to find what feels best. Lower notes often feel grounding, while higher pitches seem more energizing. Change your posture—try sitting, lying down, or resting your head on your hands as you hum.

See if you prefer humming only on the exhale or both inhale and exhale (most find exhale more natural). If being loud feels awkward, start with a whisper. For a deeper effect, especially when in pain or feeling stuck, place your hands on your chest as you hum to combine touch and sound.

Sound is personal, and shyness is common, especially if you grew up in a quiet environment. If humming around others feels odd, start quietly while waiting in line or driving. Use private spaces, such as an office or bathroom, if you want to hum louder. Humming together as a group or family can transform self-regulation into a shared, bonding ritual. Even pets often find the vibrations soothing.

Many find humming easier than other forms of breathwork, especially if anxiety makes deep breathing difficult. Focusing on vibration, not breath control, helps bypass worries about "doing it right." Musical talent isn't needed—a comfortable monotone hum is enough.

If you like structure, set a timer for two to five minutes and hum on each exhale, perhaps switching notes as you go. If your mind wanders or you feel self-conscious, refocus your attention on the vibrations in your body. Let the sound soften any tension you notice.

For those with throat sensitivity or vocal fatigue, keep humming softly and short—a little goes a long way. People with chronic pain may find that humming while lying down provides comfort, supporting relaxation in both the body and the mind.

Humming is portable—you can do it quietly almost anywhere: walking, in traffic, or at the doctor's office. Using a pillow against your chest helps muffle the sound for privacy. In groups, humming gently can foster trust and unity, making it a valuable tool for families or support groups facing challenging times.

Whether it's OM chanting, single-note singing, or gentle vowel sounds, vibration is the key, calming the nervous system by letting sound move through your body. Try different variants—what soothes you one day may not soothe you the next.

Humming is flexible, effortless, and a personal experience. With practice, you may notice that racing thoughts slow, your breath deepens naturally, and your muscles relax, even in stressful moments. It's not about performance; it's about what feels calming in your own body and voice.

Splash, Sip, Chill: Accessible Cold Exposure for Quick Relief

Sometimes, the body needs a jolt to break free from a loop of anxiety or exhaustion. One surprisingly effective reset is cold exposure—something nearly everyone can try, even without fancy equipment or extra time.

When you briefly expose your face or neck to cold, it triggers a primal reflex known as the mammalian dive reflex. This reflex instantly slows your heart rate, reduces blood pressure, and signals your nervous system to return to a state of normal alertness.

The vagus nerve plays a starring role here, carrying the message from skin to brain that it's safe to switch from "fight-or-flight" back to "rest-and-digest." You don't have to leap into an ice bath to tap this power—just a splash or a chill can do wonders.

You might be surprised by how easy it is to use cold for calm. Splashing cold water on your face is a classic trick for shaking off panic, brain fog, or a sudden wave of fatigue.

Lean over the sink, fill your hands with cold water (the colder, the better), and splash it across your forehead, cheeks, and under the eyes. Take a breath and notice the shift—your body often responds within seconds.

If you're away from home, a damp paper towel from a public restroom or even bottled cold water can serve as a substitute in a pinch.

Another option is holding something cold at the base of your neck. Grab a cold pack from the freezer, a bag of frozen veggies, or even an ice cube wrapped in a napkin.

Place it just below your hairline for 30 to 60 seconds. This area contains nerve endings that send signals directly to the vagus nerve.

The sensation can steady a racing heart and help you stay grounded during stressful moments.

If you're looking for something even more subtle—or if you're out in public—taking a small sip of ice-cold water and holding it in your mouth can create a similar effect. Let it rest on your tongue and against the roof of your mouth before swallowing.

Some people find that gently swishing the water for a few seconds adds an extra sense of refreshment, both mentally and physically. This small ritual can be useful at work, on public transportation, or anytime you need relief without drawing attention to yourself.

For those who want to take it a step further, briefly running cold water over your face or chest in the shower can amplify the effect. You don't need to drench yourself—often just 10 to 15 seconds is enough to send signals through the vagus nerve that help bring your system back toward balance.

Safety is always important when using cold exposure techniques. If you have Raynaud's syndrome (where fingers or toes turn blue or numb in cold temperatures), circulatory problems, heart conditions, or a strong sensitivity to cold, proceed with caution.

Avoid placing ice directly on bare skin for long periods, and begin with short exposures to see how your body responds. If you feel faint, overly shivery, or notice numbness that lingers, stop and warm up gradually. People living with chronic illness or frailty should check with a healthcare provider before starting regular cold exposure practices.

Cold exposure works as an on-the-spot fix for moments when anxiety spikes or when stress builds up and won't let go. You can pair these quick chills with gentle breathwork for an even more substantial effect—a "splash and breathe" mini-ritual that resets both body and mind in under two minutes.

Start by splashing your face or holding a cold object at your neck, then follow with three slow breaths out through pursed lips. Notice how the cold draws you into the present moment, and the breath helps everything settle further.

You don't need privacy or quiet for these practices—just creativity and willingness to experiment.

In an office bathroom, you can wet a paper towel with cold water and press it to your temples while taking slow breaths. At home during an anxious episode, a quick splash of water followed by a deep exhale can help break through racing thoughts or tension. Some keep a small cold pack in their work bag for emergencies. Even holding a chilled can of soda at your wrist during a stressful meeting can offer subtle relief.

For people with chronic inflammation or gut flares triggered by stress, these fast resets help interrupt the body's alarm system before symptoms spiral. Cold exposure doesn't require perfection or bravado—it's about giving yourself permission to pause and shift gears when you need it most.

Developing these "micro-practices" takes away some of the helplessness that comes with anxiety or pain flares. The next time you feel stress rising, try splashing, sipping, or chilling—and watch how quickly your system responds when given the right cue.

Vagus Nerve Self-Massage: Ears, Neck, and Jaw Release

Touch is a direct way to calm the nervous system, especially when you feel scattered or tense. Self-massage grounds you in the present and helps activate the vagus nerve's calming effects. Just a few minutes of massaging the face and neck areas can help settle nerves, ease headaches, and reduce anxiety, making these techniques particularly helpful for those with racing thoughts, jaw tension, neck stiffness, or a disconnection from their body.

Begin with your ears. The outer rim and lobes contain nerve endings connected to the vagus nerve.

Use your fingertips to slowly trace circles along each ear's rim, paying attention to the ridges and folds. Gently tug your earlobes to stretch them slightly. You might notice warmth or tingling spreading to your jaw or scalp—signs of increased parasympathetic activity. If you prefer, cover both ears with a warm washcloth first; heat softens tension and can be more comfortable if you're touch-sensitive.

Move on to your jaw and neck, which are both areas that hold stress. With your mouth slightly open, use your fingertips to gently massage the area behind the jawbone, just under the earlobe, drawing gentle circles. Continue along the jaw's edge towards your chin, using only light pressure. Next, locate the sternocleidomastoid muscle, which runs from behind the ear to the collarbone. Glide your fingers gently along it, pausing and breathing when you find tenderness, letting warmth relax the area without forcing.

If you clench or grind your teeth, releasing your jaw is important. Relax your shoulders, then gently tap along the jawline from the ears to the chin with your fingertips, allowing your jaw to hang slightly open. For a lighter touch, gently press and hold your fingertips on tense spots for a brief moment. Perform gentle, soothing movements to get effective results, without causing pain.

Why does this work? The vagus nerve branches through the neck, ears, and jaw before traveling deeper into the body.

Stimulating these areas with mindful touch activates nerve fibers that signal safety to the brain, slowing the heart rate, calming the breath, and relieving digestive upset. Nearby cranial nerves involved in chewing, swallowing, and facial expression are part of this network, so even subtle contact can shift the body from an alarm state to one of relaxation. Science supports the idea that targeted pressure and warmth at these points enhance the parasympathetic response.

If you have TMJ pain, chronic neck issues, or hand weakness, adapt these techniques.

You don't need to treat every area or stick to a set time—sometimes, just thirty seconds is beneficial. For painful gripping, use a soft massage tool or the back of an electric toothbrush (set to low, without bristles) for gentle vibration. A warm washcloth can serve as a substitute for a hand massage entirely. If movement is limited or fatigue arises, focus on one area, such as the earlobe or under the jaw, for brief sessions throughout the day.

Mindful attention deepens the benefits. Focus on sensations—feeling the skin, the pulse, the release—anchoring yourself in the moment. When thoughts intrude, redirect to physical sensations: "I feel warmth," "My jaw loosens," "I notice tingling." Combining touch and awareness can prevent stress from escalating.

There's no single proper technique. Your body will signal if more or less pressure is needed; comfort is the goal, not perfection. For many, self-massage becomes a soothing ritual, either before bed or after a stressful day.

If you manage chronic illness or fatigue, start with very short sessions. Notice how you feel after each massage, and if symptoms worsen or soreness persists, adjust the pressure or duration for the next session. For extra grounding, pair self-massage with calming music or low lighting to create a broader sense of safety.

In moments of overwhelm or pain when nothing else seems to help, self-massage offers immediate, hands-on relief. The link between gentle touch and vagus nerve activation is real and swift; for many dealing with trauma or illness-related disconnection, this simple practice offers a powerful bridge back to feeling whole.

The Power of Gargling and Gag Reflex: Surprising Tools for Calm

Gargling seems too simple—maybe even a little odd—but it can be one of the most direct ways to activate your vagus nerve and bring a wave of calm to your system. When you gargle vigorously, the muscles in your throat and soft palate work together, creating strong signals along the vagus nerve's pathway.

You don't need any special equipment or a complicated routine. All you need is a sip of water and a few moments of privacy. After brushing your teeth, fill your mouth with cool water, tilt your head back just enough to avoid swallowing, and gargle deeply. Aim for a strong bubbling sound and feel the vibration in your throat.

Continue for 15 to 30 seconds, then spit and repeat two or three times. The key is to engage the back of your throat rather than simply swishing the water around.

Why does this help? The vagus nerve branches into the throat and connects with the muscles that move when you swallow, speak, or make sounds.

When you activate these muscles through gargling, you send powerful signals to your brain that help your nervous system return to a state of low alert. It's like ringing a doorbell that signals to your body that things are safe enough to relax. This action not only interrupts stress spirals but can also improve your ability to swallow and soothe tension in the neck and jaw, two spots where anxiety loves to settle.

Some people take this a step further by using gentle stimulation of the gag reflex.That might sound intimidating, but it's not about discomfort or pushing yourself past what feels safe.

Using a clean toothbrush or tongue depressor, gently touch the very back of your tongue or the soft palate (the squishy part at the top of your mouth, just before your throat). The sensation should be brief and light, never forceful or painful. If this makes you uncomfortable or triggers a strong gag reflex, stop immediately. You're looking for mild activation, not distress.

Integrating these practices into daily life doesn't need to be awkward. Attach them to habits you already have, such as gargling after brushing your teeth in the morning or before bed.

If you're someone who feels anxious before meals or public speaking, give yourself a quick gargle in the bathroom for a confidence boost. Over time, this can become as routine as washing your face or tying your shoes. If using a tongue depressor isn't for you—or if dental work or sensitivities make it hard—skip it entirely. There's no need to force anything that feels unpleasant.

Awkwardness and embarrassment often hold people back from trying these techniques. You might feel silly making loud gargling noises if anyone's nearby. If that's you, turn on the faucet or some music to mask the sound, or choose a time when you're alone. Remember, you're doing this for your health, not to impress anyone with your technique. If even that feels like too much, humming or sipping cold water can offer similar relief with less fuss.

Gag sensitivity is common and nothing to be ashamed of—some people can't tolerate anything near the back of their mouth. Others may have dental appliances that make gargling tricky or uncomfortable. Don't push through pain or panic; instead, focus on what's accessible for you right now. Gradual exposure can help you build tolerance—start with gentle gargling for just a second or two, and gradually increase the time as it becomes easier.

Alternatives are always available if throat-focused exercises just aren't possible today. Humming softly while exhaling or sipping cold water slowly can offer similar stimulation without triggering discomfort. The most important thing is to listen to what your body needs and adjust accordingly.

These "surprising" tools may seem odd at first glance, but they open up new options for genuine relief when stress, pain, or digestive troubles arise. They're quick, portable, and easy to fit into even the busiest routine—no meditation cushion required.

As we close out this chapter on rapid-access tools for calming your nervous system, remember that these practices are invitations to reconnect with safety in simple ways—through sound, touch, temperature, and now even gargling. Every technique is another way to tell your body, "You're safe." Next, we'll explore building daily routines that stack these small wins into lasting resilience and deeper wellness.

A quick Optional Note

IF YOU'RE FINDING PARTS of this book helpful, you're welcome to move through it at whatever pace feels right for you. There's no need to read everything in order or try every exercise. Following what feels supportive in your body matters more than completing anything.

If at some point—now or later—you feel like sharing your experience, you're welcome to leave a short review. Reviews can help others living with chronic pain find this book and decide whether it might support them. Leaving a review is entirely optional.

If you'd like to share your thoughts, you can leave a review on Amazon.

When you're ready, continue to the next section.

Chapter 6

Building Daily Routines for Lasting Resilience

Morning Nervous System Priming: Start Your Day in "Rest-and-Digest"

Mornings often feel overwhelming before you even get up—your mind may race with worries, your body aches, or your gut feels unsettled. Many people with anxiety, trauma, chronic pain, or sleep issues find mornings especially tough, and the first moments of the day can feel like a struggle.

I've seen people, including loved ones, go through mornings like this, where just getting out of bed feels exhausting. It's easy to let stress dictate the tone of your day, but there are simple ways to reclaim your mornings and give your body a head start on a calm day.

You don't need complicated, lengthy routines. True nervous system shifts come from simple practices repeated with consistency. Taking just three to five minutes can significantly alter the trajectory of your entire day.

The key is gently signaling your body that "rest-and-digest" is the default, not fight-or-flight. You don't have to wake up extra early or add major tasks; try pairing one or two calming actions with things you already do, like sitting up after your alarm or washing your face. Aim for repetition, not perfection—even a few mindful breaths count.

A routine should fit your life and energy. If you're a parent, your window might be before the kids wake or as coffee brews. Night-shift workers may have their "morning" at 2 pm, which is fine, too. Students could try a routine as their computer boots up. The key is to make these minutes yours—a small gift to your nervous system, not just another obligation.

A gentle sequence might begin with sitting at the edge of the bed, with your feet on the ground. Take three slow breaths, making each exhale a bit longer than the inhale. If breathwork is too much, hum a low "mmm" sound, which vibrates your chest and throat and calms the vagus nerve.

Next, use your fingertips to gently massage around your ears and jaw to release the night's tension—no need for deep pressure, just a gentle waking up of those nerves. If pressed for time, hum while brushing your teeth or massage your neck while waiting for the shower to warm up.

Finish with a moment of intention or gratitude. Notice something you're thankful for—a cozy blanket, a pet, or the feel of your breath. Some people choose a word for the day—such as calm, steady, or open—or quietly affirm, "I am starting my day with calm and intention." Pairing a thought like this with a physical action helps ground it in your mind and body.

Starting your day in "rest-and-digest" has real effects. It allows your nervous system to reset after sleep or nightmares, lowers your baseline anxiety, aids digestion, and prepares you to face stressful moments—such as emails, school chaos, or commutes—with steadier energy. Over time, you may find that minor setbacks affect you less, and your gut settles more easily after meals.

Forming new habits isn't easy, especially when pain, fatigue, or anxiety intervene overnight. On tough days, prep a "morning calm kit" before bed: leave a reminder note on your nightstand, set out your favorite scent nearby, or place a cozy sweater where you'll see it. If you miss a day or only manage a quick practice, remember that even brief moments help. Every small effort builds resilience.

Interactive Element: Morning Calm Kit Checklist

- Sticky reminder on your alarm or phone
- Soft scarf or favorite sweater for a gentle touch
- Essential oil (like lavender) near where you get dressed
- One gratitude or intention written on an index card
- A calming morning "soundtrack" song
- A glass of water is ready for hydration

Choose one or two favorites—simplicity works. The goal isn't to impress but to tell your body that calm is its priority. Each time you return to this routine, even imperfectly, you help strengthen your resilience from within.

"Micro-Calm Moments" for Busy Days: 1-Minute Practices on the Go

There's a common myth that healing or nervous system care requires big chunks of time, perfect conditions, or silence—but life usually doesn't allow for that.

Living with anxiety, trauma, chronic pain, or gut issues often means unpredictable schedules where it's hard to find even a moment to breathe. That's where micro-calming comes in: quick, potent practices—each a minute or less—that fit anywhere into your day—no need for a yoga mat, quiet room, or privacy. What matters is incorporating these moments regularly, not how long they last.

Micro-calming involves short, intentional pauses to activate your vagus nerve and release tension, even amid chaos.

These mini-practices build resilience over time, gradually rewiring your nervous system through consistency rather than perfection or lengthy routines. Each time you hum at a red light or massage your jaw during a bathroom break, you're signaling safety to your body and interrupting the stress cycle.

Start by identifying your "stress hotspots"—moments when tension usually spikes, like sitting in traffic, walking into work, folding laundry, waiting in line, or after a tough phone call.

Once you find these, pair a micro-calm technique with each one. For example, if meetings leave you jittery, try humming as you walk to the conference room. If phone calls make you anxious, squeeze in a quick ear massage while on mute or after you hang up.

Here are quick, 1-minute practices for various settings:

- **Hum quietly** while driving or walking. Keep your lips closed and notice the buzz in your chest or throat. This hum soothes the vagus nerve discreetly.

- **Box breathing** while waiting—inhale for four counts, hold for four, exhale for four, hold for four. This balanced breath calms your heart and mind.
- **Ear or jaw massage** during bathroom breaks. Use gentle circles on your outer ear or along your jawline to quickly settle tension.
- **Cold water reset**: If you're washing your hands or face, let cold water linger on your wrists or cheeks for a few breaths—a quick, sensory way to ground and calm yourself.
- **Lengthen your exhale** in a checkout line or at your desk—make it twice as long as your inhale to quietly calm racing thoughts.
- **Sip and swish cold water** during parenting chaos to give yourself a brief nervous system "reset" and promote a calmer response.
- **Tactile grounding** in noisy, crowded spaces—press your thumb to each fingertip while breathing slowly for subtle, powerful grounding.

Making these moments automatic takes reminders and cues. Set phone alarms with a calming phrase, or place sticky notes in frequent spots, such as your water bottle or bathroom mirror, to help you stay focused and on task. Stack micro-calms onto routines: hum as you wash your hands, breathe deeply after every email, or massage your ear during coffee breaks.

Pair your chosen practice with something you already do daily (habit-stacking), like riding the bus or checking social media, to make integrating micro-calming easier and more consistent.

Remember, it's not about "doing it right." Some days you'll forget, and other days you'll only manage a single breath before moving on. That's fine—each slight pause is like saving for the future. Over weeks and months, your nervous system gradually adapts to new patterns of safety and calm.

Micro-calming is a lifeline if you're too busy or overwhelmed for longer self-care routines. Even those with chronic pain or fatigue can usually spare a minute or two. Over time, these practices become a natural way to manage stress and unpredictability, rather than an additional thing to worry about.

Many people with demanding schedules find these mini rituals bring real progress—less reactivity at work, fewer flare-ups on stressful afternoons, more patience at home. All it takes is permitting yourself to pause for just a minute.

Experiment to find what works best for you. The more often you use micro-calms, the more instinctive and effective they become, helping you stay resilient, even on the most chaotic days.

Bedtime Wind-Down: Routines for Deep, Restorative Sleep

Winding down at night can be tough, especially if anxiety, trauma, pain, or gut issues flare as soon as you lie down. Many people become trapped in cycles of racing thoughts, tense bodies, and restlessness, even when they are exhausted. You are not alone—nights are often hardest for those with high stress, health challenges, or emotional wounds.

A nightly routine isn't about more pressure or creating another thing to fail at. Instead, it sends your nervous system a signal: "It's safe to rest now." The aim isn't perfect sleep or immediate results, but instead a gradual transition before bed. Think of it as a gentle ramp, giving your brain and body time to switch gears, especially after a hyper-alert day. Even ten minutes of focused winding down can gradually help.

Start about twenty minutes before bed, but don't worry if you only have ten or five—it still helps. Dim your home lights to signal your brain that night has come. Avoid blue light from screens and, if possible, switch to warmer lighting. Try adding a sensory cue, such as dabbing a bit of lavender oil on your palms or near your bed, and taking a deep breath—this signals to your vagus nerve that it's time to slow down.

Settle into bed or a comfy chair. Try gently humming or chanting soft sounds ("mmm" or "om") as you exhale. You don't need musical talent; the vibration through your chest and throat calms the vagus nerve, easing the switch to "rest-and-digest." Continue for a few minutes, noticing your breath and how your muscles relax. Next, breathe softly: inhale through your nose for four counts, exhale slowly for eight counts. If thoughts distract you, gently return your attention to your breath and the release that occurs with each exhale.

Warmth amplifies calm. Place a warm cloth on your neck or chest to relax the muscles and ease tension. If you like to touch, gently massage your ears or trace your jawline with your fingertips—these nerves relate to the vagus nerve and can help release stress.

Create a cocooning environment. Weighted blankets provide comforting pressure, signaling safety to your nervous system. Soft background sounds—such as nature noises, gentle music, or a fan—can help block out distractions and foster a sense of calm. Choose whatever makes your space feel safe and inviting.

If insomnia or anxiety keeps disrupting your nights, remember: it's not a personal failing. Some bodies—especially those of shift workers or parents—resist sleep due to disrupted sleep patterns or unpredictable demands. Adapt your routine: hum while rocking a baby, practice slow breathing during breaks, or fit in what you can, even if interrupted. Partial routines still help calm your system.

When sleep won't come, remind yourself that the routine is helping, even if you're awake longer than hoped. Calming techniques lower cortisol levels, reduce muscle tension, and gradually retrain your body to expect nighttime safety rather than dread. Reassure yourself: "Do what you can, when you can." Some nights will be harder, but setbacks don't erase progress.

If frustration or spiraling thoughts rise, pause for self-compassion: place a hand on your heart or belly, feel its warmth, breathe deeply, and offer kind words to yourself—even silently. Sometimes sleep is elusive despite effort; what matters most is the willingness to care for yourself.

If you live with chronic pain or nighttime gut issues, keep routines gentle and flexible. Lying on your side with a pillow between your knees may help ease breathing discomfort; try different positions or sensory cues until you find what soothes you.

Lastly, make bedtime rituals something you look forward to. Pick scents or sounds you love, shorten routines when tired, and celebrate any moment of ease you notice—even if brief. You're not just chasing sleep; you're rebuilding trust with your nervous system after years of disruption—each night's effort plants seeds for future rest.

Symptom-Based Menus: Picking the Right Exercise for Your Needs

When your body feels off, starting can be tough. Anxiety might spike unexpectedly, or digestive issues and sleeplessness can hit out of nowhere.

There's no universal fix—what calms you one day may not help the next. That's why a "choose-your-own-relief" menu—personalized by the symptoms you feel in the moment—can be a game changer. Use these menus as a toolkit: organized, accessible, and tailored to your current needs, so you don't have to recall every technique on the spot.

Begin by asking yourself, "What am I experiencing?" Naming your symptom opens doors to specific relief.

For example, if your heart races and your hands shake, that's classic anxiety. Stomach cramps or bloating after eating mean gut distress. Sudden pain flares or a creeping headache signal other patterns. Each symptom triggers your nervous system differently, and specific vagus nerve exercises target those particular responses.

For anxiety and restlessness, breathwork is especially effective. Try slow, deep inhales and longer exhales until the tension begins to ease. Quiet humming or pressing fingertips along your jaw can also break up tension and signal calm through the vagus nerve.

If panic hits in public, discreet humming or a gentle ear massage can help without attracting attention. You only need a minute and a bit of privacy.

Gut discomfort responds to other approaches. If you're bloated or cramped, sip cold water and hold it in your mouth briefly; pair this with slow breathing (inhale through the nose for four counts, exhale through pursed lips for eight). Massaging around your ears or rubbing your neck can aid digestion and ease discomfort. These quick tactics work discreetly, even in the workplace or at school.

Pain flares need grounding and gentle touch. For sudden aches, use a warm compress on your neck or gently massage your temples and jaw. Low-pitch humming may relieve migraines or facial pain by relaxing tense muscles. If pain keeps you stuck, focus on breathwork with longer exhales, or visualize warmth spreading through tense spots as you breathe.

Sleep issues have their own set of tools. When you're sleepless, begin with slow, exhale breathing while lying down, focusing on the heaviness of your body against the mattress. Two or three minutes of humming can cue your brain to settle. Add an ear massage or a hand on your heart to further calm racing thoughts.

For work stress—whether during meetings or after difficult conversations—have a rapid response plan: try discreet humming, massage your ear under the table, or splash cool water on your face during a quick break. If you can't leave, slow box breathing (inhale-hold-exhale-hold for four counts each) can effectively calm stress without being noticed.

Your preferences will change. What helps during one panic attack may not help during the next; sometimes touch soothes, while at other times it's overwhelming. That's why it's helpful to keep notes—a small notebook or phone app entry will do. Write what you tried, what worked, and how you felt after. Over time, you'll build a menu that's ideally suited to your needs and experiences.

If you like visuals or want something more interactive, you can create a simple chart—either printed or digital—with columns for your main symptoms, such as anxiety, gut trouble, pain flares, sleep difficulties, or work stress. Under each one, list a few go-to practices that help in the moment.

For example, during an anxiety spike, you might use humming or a slow exhale; for gut discomfort, a sip of cold water or gentle neck massage; for pain flares, a warm compress or low-pitch humming; for sleep struggles, ear massage or box breathing; and for work stress, something discreet like an ear rub or a splash of cold water. Keep it simple and easy to update.

Treat this as a living guide. Add new techniques as you discover what works, and adjust them as your needs change over time. Relief shifts with your body, your environment, and your energy—it doesn't stay fixed.

As you keep using these tools, patterns will start to stand out. You might notice that humming helps before a stressful conversation, or that cold water settles your stomach after meals. That kind of awareness is real progress.

This guide is yours—shape it in a way that supports you, moment by moment.

Tracking Progress: Using Mood, Digestion, and Sleep Logs

When you're working hard to change old patterns—especially if you're living with anxiety, trauma, pain, gut troubles, or sleep issues—progress can feel invisible. You might wonder if any of these new routines are helping.

One of the best ways to break through that fog is by tracking your experience. Simple logs for mood, digestion, sleep, and energy turn vague impressions into something you can see and reflect on. For many people, this is the first moment they begin to feel hope that things can shift, even if only a little at a time.

You don't need fancy journals or expensive apps. A basic notebook, a note on your phone, or even a printable template taped to your fridge works just fine.

Keep it simple and doable: jot down how you feel each morning and night, track how digestion feels after meals, mark your sleep quality, or note your energy levels during the day. If you enjoy technology, apps like Daylio or Bearable can make tracking quick and visual. Some people prefer symbols—like a sun for a good day or a cloud for a hard one—while others use numbers or a few short words. The important thing is choosing a method that fits easily into your life.

As you record entries over days and weeks, patterns often begin to appear. After a couple of weeks of gentle evening breathwork, falling asleep becomes easier. Or a simple log may reveal that your gut symptoms worsen after stressful days but improve when you practice even a short humming routine.

These small observations matter. Moments when you bounce back faster after a rough day or need fewer stomach medications during the week are signs of progress. The symptoms may not disappear overnight, but improvement often happens in small steps. Look for the subtle wins: a night with less pain, a calmer response during an argument, or a morning where your energy lasts longer than usual.

Logs aren't just about improvement—they're valuable when things don't go as planned. If you see sleep improving but mood stays low, maybe it's time to tweak your evening routine or add a midday micro-calm practice. If digestive trouble flares up after certain meals or stressful events, that's valuable data.

Adjust your routines based on these clues: consider trying more breath-work before lunch or adding a short self-massage after work. The log turns frustration into information—a way to advocate for yourself and tailor your routines to your needs.

It's normal for tracking to bring up mixed feelings. On tough weeks, you might look at your log and feel like nothing's working or get discouraged by setbacks.

If this happens, remember that healing is rarely a linear process. Some days will be harder, and progress may stall or even reverse. Logs are for understanding, not for blame or chasing perfection. Their actual value is showing how you respond over time, not just whether symptoms disappear.

To keep things motivating (and not overwhelming), keep log entries brief—a sentence or two is enough. For example: "Woke up tired but slept through the night," "Felt less anxious after lunch today," or "Stomach cramps after work stress."

Once a month, review your notes and highlight any positive changes, no matter how small. Maybe your recovery time after stress has shrunk from two days to one. That's worth recognizing.

Here are a few sample entries from people who've used logs to guide their routines:

- "Felt anxious this morning but calmed down quickly after humming."
- "Had heartburn after dinner; tried slow breathing before bed—felt better."
- "Energy higher all week; only one bad pain flare."
- "Fell asleep faster three nights in a row."

If tracking feels like too much or starts to create pressure, it's okay to pause or scale back. Log only what feels meaningful—maybe just three words each night—or return to it when you're ready. The tool is there to support you, not to create another obligation.

Over time, these simple records become a powerful tool for self-advocacy. You'll be able to share trends with doctors or therapists, explain what works for your body, and make informed choices about what to try next. The goal isn't perfection—it's building awareness and celebrating any forward movement, no matter how small.

As this chapter comes to a close, remember that daily routines and honest reflection go hand in hand. With tracking as your ally, those subtle signs of healing become more visible. Every entry counts toward building resilience and learning what truly supports you, one day at a time. Up next: we'll explore how to personalize and adapt these practices as life and symptoms change, making lasting calm more than just a wish.

Chapter 7

Personalizing Your Healing: Adapting to Your Body, Triggers, and Life

Customizing Routines for Anxiety, Trauma, Sleep, and Gut Issues

Symptoms can fluctuate daily—one day it's gut discomfort, another day it's trouble sleeping or managing anxiety. Healing isn't about rigid routines but about responding honestly to what your body needs in the moment.

Many mainstream wellness plans overlook how unpredictable symptoms can be—anxiety before work, trauma memories surfacing unexpectedly, or sleep problems after a stressful day. Because nervous systems differ, rigid routines often fall short.

The most effective approach is flexible and modular. Instead of following a single fixed routine, you can combine techniques depending on what you're experiencing. Over time, this becomes a personal toolkit shaped by your own patterns and lived experience.

Begin by identifying your top symptoms—for example, morning dread, evening restlessness, gut pain, or trauma triggers. Use your symptom tracker or jot down your main two or three challenges. What flares up most—anxiety before meetings, sleeplessness after a tough day, or gut pain at lunch?

Once you know your priorities, select routines that align with them. For anxiety, try slow breathing and humming before stressful events. If trauma feels intense, create a safe space with grounding objects, gentle movement, and comforting touch.

For sleep, build a wind-down ritual: long exhale breaths in dim lighting, a gentle ear massage, and a dark, quiet room. Gut discomfort may respond to pre-meal breathwork, a cold sip of water after eating, and resting a warm hand on your abdomen.

Adapting these routines to your day is key. Don't force morning practices if you're groggy or rushed—try them at lunch or later in the day. Your routines don't need to be long; you can break a ten-minute sequence into shorter bits. Anchor practices at times when you have the most energy or need the most support, like evenings or stressful afternoons.

Adjust intensity: do the whole routine on good days, and scale back to a breath or a hum on tougher ones. Being flexible isn't just helpful—it's crucial for sustainable healing.

Think of these routines like "recipe cards" you can shuffle based on what you need most.

For anxiety before social events: two minutes of slow breathing and quiet humming in a private spot. For trauma after difficult moments: use a soft blanket, grounding objects, gentle neck rolls, and deep breaths.

For restless sleep, try the following: massage your ears in bed, take five slow breaths, dim the room, and play a calming noise. For gut tension: three deep belly breaths before eating, cold water after, and a comforting hand on your stomach.

Journaling is essential. Use your logs to notice what helps you recover or feel better. You may discover that humming before meetings is more effective than breathwork alone, or that pre-meal routines help alleviate bloating. Annotate your routines as you go: "Calm after humming," "Slept better with ear massage," "Less pain with breathwork." Over time, you'll see patterns and refine your approach, making each week's routine more tailored and effective for you.

Build-Your-Own Routine Table

Create your own table to experiment and track which methods work best. Swap techniques as your needs shift. Look for patterns over several weeks rather than day by day.

Personalizing your practices makes healing sustainable, rather than another broken promise. Use your logs to highlight small wins, refine your routines, and recognize progress, such as recovering from setbacks more quickly or sleeping a bit longer. Each improvement is genuine and unique to you—no generic program can offer this kind of personalized progress.

What If You Feel Worse? Troubleshooting and Gentle Alternatives

Sometimes, when you try something new for your nervous system, things don't go as planned. Maybe you feel lightheaded during breathwork, or a wave of emotion—such as sadness or anger—suddenly rises. Some people notice new aches, tingling, or discomfort in areas that didn't bother them before.

If this happens, it isn't a sign of failure or proof that something is wrong with you. These reactions are common and understandable. Years of stress or trauma can make the nervous system sensitive to unfamiliar change, even when that change intends to help.

It can feel like turning on the lights in a dark room. Everything suddenly looks different, and that shift can feel uncomfortable at first. What's happening is that your body is adjusting, sometimes pushing back as old patterns meet new signals.

Instead of forcing your way through the experience, slow everything down and permit yourself to pause.

Discomfort can show up in different ways. Some people feel dizzy or short of breath when practicing deep breathing exercises. Others cry or experience waves of emotion they can't explain. At times, a practice meant to help you relax may leave you feeling agitated or unsettled.

This kind of nervous system "pushback" isn't unusual—it often appears when the body begins learning new ways to regulate. It doesn't mean you're doing something wrong. It means your system is responding, even if the response feels confusing or messy. If a technique sets off alarm bells, stop right away. There's no reward for pushing through distress.

A troubleshooting mindset can help you move through these bumps with less fear. Start by adjusting the intensity or length of the exercise. If five minutes of breathwork feels overwhelming, try one or two minutes instead. Sometimes less truly works better.

If breath-holding makes you dizzy or uneasy, focus only on longer exhales and skip breath-holds entirely. When a practice repeatedly triggers discomfort, try a different approach. If breathwork doesn't feel right, experiment with humming, gentle touch, or calming sounds instead.

For people who find sound overwhelming, shift to texture. Hold a smooth stone, trace the lines in your palm with your thumb, or notice the feel of a soft fabric. Ground yourself before and after exercises: plant your feet on the floor, feel the weight of your body in the chair, or quietly name what you see around you.

Some days feel too heavy for active exercises. On those days, gentler options can help. Mindful hand holding—wrapping one hand around the other and noticing the warmth—can steady your system when it feels shaky.

Tracing the outline of each finger with the opposite hand also works as a subtle grounding practice. You can also use scent to support calm: apply a favorite essential oil or scented lotion to your wrist and inhale slowly.

When everything feels overwhelming, pause and observe. Notice your breath without trying to change it, listen for distant sounds, or feel the texture of your clothing against your skin. These quiet moments of observation can interrupt spirals without asking too much energy from you.

You don't have to push your limits to heal. Honoring them is a crucial form of self-respect. Healing means listening to your body's whispers before they become shouts. If pausing an exercise leads to relief, consider that a sign of progress. Sometimes, stopping is the bravest thing you can do. If distress sticks around—like panic that won't settle, flashbacks, or overwhelming sadness—reach out to a trauma-informed therapist or supportive friend. No shame belongs here; needing more support is not a weakness, but rather a sign of wisdom.

A gentle affirmation for days like this: "Pausing is progress, not giving up." You're allowed to take breaks and adapt every practice to fit what feels possible today. If you're ever unsure if an exercise is safe for you—maybe because of a medical condition, psychiatric symptoms, or something else—ask a healthcare provider for guidance. You deserve safety as much as relief.

Healing isn't about powering through every practice or getting instant results. It's about responding honestly to what your body says right now. Small steps forward count just as much as big leaps. On rougher days, choosing rest or comfort over intensity is an act of trust in yourself—a step toward steadier ground without shame or apology.

Overcoming "Too Busy" and Sticking with Your Practice

Life often fills every moment, and adding anything—even healing routines—can seem impossible. With packed calendars, self-care or nervous system routines may feel out of reach, especially for those already dealing with anxiety, trauma, pain, or gut issues.

You might feel guilty wanting more time or resentful at the suggestion that healing requires a perfect schedule. However, nervous system care doesn't require complicated rituals or large time blocks—it can be as simple as quick, everyday habits.

Think of vagus nerve practice as brief, frequent drops rather than occasional long showers. Tiny habits—actions that take less than a minute—can add up, much like brushing your teeth. You already perform dozens of small tasks each day, so the key is to attach calming exercises to the things you already do.

Focus on transition points—those brief pauses between activities when your mind naturally resets. Moments like waking up, waiting for coffee, taking a bathroom break, or walking to your car can become small opportunities for regulation. Even thirty seconds can help. Use those moments for a slow breath, a quiet hum, or a gentle ear massage.

Daily chores also offer natural openings to care for your nervous system. You might hum while washing dishes or folding laundry. Try a short self-massage while listening to a podcast or watching television.

Breathwork can pair easily with a short walk or while waiting at a red light. Some people hold a smooth stone during phone calls as a grounding touchpoint, or hum softly while drafting emails or waiting on hold. The goal is to weave these practices into everyday life so they feel natural rather than like another task on your to-do list.

If you lean toward perfectionism or all-or-nothing thinking, remember that no one grades your nervous system work. You don't have to complete every step every day or follow a strict order. There's no penalty for shortening a practice or skipping one entirely.

Real change often begins when you allow yourself to practice imperfectly and focus on effort rather than outcomes. Something is always better than nothing. Even one minute of breathwork matters, and missing a day or two doesn't erase your progress.

Consistency helps, but rigid adherence isn't necessary. The nervous system responds to repetition over time, not to perfect streaks.

Mindset plays an important role. If you catch yourself thinking, "I failed because I missed my routine today," try reframing it: "I took a few deep breaths while making tea, and that helped."

Celebrate those small wins. Some days will feel messier than others, especially when symptoms flare or life becomes busy. On difficult days, any act of self-care—no matter how small—deserves recognition. You're building resilience, not perfection.

Since motivation can be fleeting, utilize tools to support your new habits. Printable habit trackers—with stickers or checkboxes—can be surprisingly motivating; seeing progress makes it more tangible. Place your tracker in a visible location, such as on the fridge. For extra support, find a "calm buddy"—someone who also wants to focus on nervous system care. Texting quick check-ins keeps you accountable and removes isolation.

Rewards matter, even small ones. Choose meaningful ways to celebrate milestones: a new candle after a week of practice, a long bath after five days, or guilt-free TV time after evening breathwork. The size of the reward isn't essential—just that it feels satisfying to you.

Changing your environment can also help. Place a sticky note on the mirror ("exhale slow"), set a phone alarm ("hum break"), or keep a massage tool at your desk. Visible cues are silent prompts to practice.

Over time, these micro-practices blend into your daily routine, requiring less mental energy and becoming automatic. You may hum before tense calls or massage your jaw while watching TV without needing a reminder.

These moments accumulate, gradually shifting your baseline from constant tension to calmer steadiness.

Most importantly, keep things simple, gentle, and let go of perfectionism. Life is busy enough—choose practices that fit your real world, not an idealized version of you.

Combining Vagus Nerve Exercises with Therapy, Medication, or Other Modalities

Integrating vagus nerve exercises with therapy, medication, or other healing methods can enhance your daily well-being. These practices often work best alongside other forms of support, helping create a steadier and more balanced healing process.

Whether you are in therapy, taking medication, or exploring holistic approaches, you can incorporate vagus nerve routines into your overall care. There's no need to keep them separate. Many therapists and doctors appreciate it when people become actively involved in caring for their own health.

At the same time, it's natural to wonder whether these exercises could interfere with your current treatment or require extra caution. Your safety and comfort should always come first.

Begin by discussing your interest in vagus nerve practices with your healthcare provider. Starting the conversation promotes collaboration and keeps everyone informed about your self-care efforts. If you're unsure how to bring it up, you might say, "I've been reading about vagus nerve exercises for anxiety (or sleep, gut issues, etc.). Is there anything I should consider as I add these?" You could also ask, "I'd like to include some self-regulation routines between sessions—could you help me adapt them to my treatment?"

Honest conversation protects your safety and often opens the door to helpful guidance from your therapist or doctor. They may offer suggestions for integrating these practices into your current care.

If you take medication for anxiety, depression, chronic pain, or inflammation, vagus nerve exercises do not chemically interact with those medications. Still, they may support a greater sense of stability. Some people notice their medications feel more effective when paired with consistent self-regulation practices.

For those in talk therapy, vagus nerve routines can make emotionally challenging sessions feel more manageable. They can help you ground yourself more quickly and recover after discussing difficult memories or experiences. Therapy helps build understanding, while nervous system practices help the body feel safer during emotional work.

Some health conditions require extra caution. If you have a heart rhythm disorder, epilepsy, or severe psychiatric symptoms such as psychosis or active suicidality, consult your healthcare provider before starting new practices—especially those involving breath retention, cold exposure, or vigorous movement.

People with Raynaud's syndrome should avoid cold-water techniques and choose gentler options, such as humming or slow breathing. Individuals with breathing conditions such as asthma or COPD should approach deep breathing or breath-holding carefully and focus on shorter, gentler breathing cycles instead.

During therapy or support groups, communicate what works and what doesn't. Let your provider know if something feels good or brings discomfort. For instance, say, "The grounding exercise we used last time really helped; could we do it again if I get overwhelmed?" or, "I sometimes get dizzy with breathwork—could we use touch or sound cues instead?" These dialogues make the process safer and more supportive.

Combining modalities often creates multiplied benefits. For example, someone managing panic attacks with medication might see a reduced need for emergency doses by adding daily slow breathing and humming. In trauma therapy, simple grounding touch before and after sessions may ease residual distress.

Nutrition and movement matter too—eating gut-friendly foods with pre-meal breathwork can improve both digestion and mood. At the same time, gentle movement, combined with vagus nerve activation, can relieve pain and calm the mind.

Personal stories illustrate these benefits: one reader paired evening sleep medication with a short ear massage routine and found her sleep deeper and more restorative. Another practice was humming after weekly therapy to retain insights without feeling emotionally drained.

These aren't just anecdotes—studies show that people who support their nervous system using a variety of techniques often experience better results than those who use only one approach. The goal isn't to add more tasks, but to weave together simple practices that reinforce one another.

If your care team isn't familiar with vagus nerve work, that's okay. You can share resources or describe the exercises you're using. Many providers are open to learning, especially if it helps you stay motivated and optimistic in recovery.

Most importantly, listen to your body. If anything—whether it's a medicine, therapy technique, or self-regulation exercise—that feels off or uncomfortable, pause and seek guidance. Healing is personal, and you deserve care that honors every aspect of your well-being.

Building Trust in Your Body Again: Celebrating Small Wins

Living with anxiety, trauma, inflammation, or unpredictable health symptoms can leave you feeling like your own body is a stranger, sometimes even an enemy. The real challenge isn't just the symptoms—pain that appears uninvited, sleepless nights, or a gut that rebels without warning—but the sense that you can't rely on your own body.

When flare-ups appear unexpectedly, or old trauma gets triggered by something as simple as a scent or a sound, it's easy to lose trust in yourself. Many people describe feeling betrayed by their own bodies, as if stability might disappear at any moment. The fear of another setback can make you brace for impact even on better days.

Regaining trust rarely happens overnight. It grows slowly as you begin noticing, supporting, and acknowledging what your body does right—even if that progress lasts only a minute or two.

One of the most meaningful shifts begins when you notice small changes instead of waiting for dramatic milestones. You might sleep thirty minutes longer than usual one night. Perhaps you catch yourself just before spiraling into panic and use a slow breath or a grounding touch to steady yourself.

These moments can feel tiny, almost invisible, but they signal that something is changing beneath the surface. Your nervous system is beginning to respond, even if only in brief flashes.

Writing these moments down can help make progress visible. Record details such as "Woke up with less pain today," "Laughed with my partner before dinner," or "Felt my stomach relax after lunch." Over time, these notes become evidence that healing isn't just possible—it's already happening in small ways.

Creating simple rituals can also help you recognize progress. One option is a "progress jar." Whenever you notice an improvement, write it on a small piece of paper and place it in the jar.

Maybe you made it through a stressful meeting without feeling overwhelmed, or you enjoyed a meal without gut pain. At the end of each week or month, read through the notes as a reminder that real change is unfolding.

You can also use reflection prompts such as "What felt different this week?" or "When did I feel calm, even for a moment?" Questions like these gently guide your attention toward what is quietly improving.

If you belong to a support group or have a trusted friend walking a similar path, consider sharing your small victories. Sometimes speaking them aloud helps make progress feel more real and less fleeting.

Self-compassion is the glue that holds this process together. When symptoms return, or progress seem to stall, it's easy to fall into self-blame or frustration. Rebuilding trust with your body takes patience and kindness, along with the understanding that progress rarely moves in a straight line.

Some days will feel as though everything is slipping backward. Those moments can be discouraging, but they don't erase the progress you've already made. A helpful reminder during those times is simple: "Every step counts, even the tiny ones."

A body gratitude practice can help anchor this mindset. Each morning or evening, take a moment to name one part of your body that you appreciate—your hands for their strength, your eyes for noticing beauty, or your legs for carrying you through the day.

Over time, this practice can shift your relationship with your body, replacing resentment with a growing sense of partnership.

It's also worth noticing how setbacks often bring hidden lessons. Perhaps a relapse reveals a new trigger or uncovers an exercise that proves more effective than expected. Instead of seeing these dips as failures, try viewing them as information—data points guiding you toward what works best for you right now.

This reframing takes the sting out of tough days and keeps you engaged with the process, rather than checking out due to disappointment. Healing isn't about erasing all symptoms or achieving perfect health; it's about finding more moments where your body feels like home again.

Building trust in your body doesn't mean feeling anxious, tired, or uncomfortable again. It means noticing when ease returns—even briefly—and letting yourself celebrate it instead of brushing it off as luck or coincidence.

Over time, these small wins accumulate, creating a record of resilience that you can look back on when doubt creeps in. You may find yourself responding to stress differently, bouncing back faster after flare-ups, or simply feeling more at ease within your skin. These steady changes form the foundation for more profound healing and lasting calm.

In closing this chapter, remember that every note in your progress jar and every gentle reflection matter more than you think. Small wins are not just signs of hope—they are the building blocks of restored trust and steady healing. As we move forward, keep these celebrations close and stay curious about what else your body can do when given patience and support. Next up, we'll explore how to integrate vagus nerve work into broader wellness habits for even greater balance and resilience.

Chapter 8

Gentle Somatic Movement for Vagus Nerve Activation

SOME DAYS, YOUR BODY feels not just tired, but stuck in a holding pattern. If you feel disconnected from your body, overwhelmed, or "off," know that others share this experience as well. Often, the idea of exercising feels out of reach, especially when anxiety, trauma, pain, or chronic illness weighs you down. But healing doesn't demand effort or strain—slow, mindful movement offers a way to soothe and reconnect your body, focusing on safety and calm rather than flexibility or fitness. This approach isn't about perfect poses or breaking a sweat; it's about working gently with your nervous system, using movement as an invitation to relax and regulate.

Somatic movement—and even simple forms of gentle stretching—can subtly but powerfully stimulate your vagus nerve. Slow, intentional motion sends signals of safety to the body: sensors in your muscles and joints sense gentle stretch and relay that information to the brain. This feedback loop helps calm the stress response and supports your body's ability to recover from stress.

It isn't just about what you do, but how you do it. Mindful breathing, slow movement, and attention to sensation create the conditions your nervous system needs to shift out of "high alert." Simple posture changes—such as sitting upright, rolling your shoulders back, or turning your head—also play a role, allowing these small adjustments to influence the body more broadly.

Here are some simple, adaptable sequences that can bring steadiness and ease, no matter your pain, energy level, or mobility:

- **Seated Cat-Cow:** Sit with feet on the floor and hands on thighs. Breathe in as you gently arch your back and open your chest. Breathe out as you round your spine and lower your chin toward your chest. Move slowly, matching breath to movement. Even gentle spinal movement helps wake up the spine, massages the gut, and stimulates vagus nerve pathways.

- **Reclined Twist:** Lying on your back with knees bent, let your knees fall to one side. In contrast, your head turns in the opposite direction.

Take several slow breaths, feeling the stretch through your belly and spine. This pose soothes tense muscles and promotes relaxation by stimulating vagus nerve fibers along the core. If lying down isn't possible, try a twist in bed or while seated, turning your upper body while keeping your hips forward.

- **Supported Child's Pose:** Kneel or sit at the edge of a bed, then fold forward over a pillow or blanket. Let arms drape or rest at your side. Focus on lengthening your out-breath, which further relaxes the nervous system and helps relieve racing thoughts or sleeplessness.

- **Gentle Neck Rolls:** Seated upright, relax your shoulders. On an exhale, lower your right ear to your right shoulder, then roll your chin to your chest and over to the left shoulder. Move gently, pausing if you feel tension or dizziness. Match movement to your breath. Gentle neck rolls can help ease headaches, jaw tension, and stress, as the vagus nerve runs near the side of the neck.

Chair-based variations and ample support (such as pillows under your knees or behind your back, or folded blankets under your feet) make every movement accessible, regardless of your strength or energy level. Modify as needed: use smaller movements, provide more support, and take longer rests. If any position feels unsafe (such as eyes closed or lying flat), adjust or skip it. Your comfort and sense of safety are essential for healing.

Try It Yourself: Gentle Vagus Flow Checklist

- Seated cat-cow (2–3 slow rounds)
- Reclined or seated twist (each side, 3–5 slow breaths)
- Supported child's pose or forward fold (1–2 minutes)
- Gentle neck rolls (1–2 slow circles each way)

Use props as you need, rest often, and skip anything that doesn't feel good.

Remember: this practice is about listening to your body, not pushing through discomfort. Every mindful movement sends a message of safety, letting your nervous system know it can return to calm when life gets loud.

Heart Rate Variability Biofeedback: A Guide for Home Use

Reading your body's signals can be tricky, especially when stress or fatigue clouds your sense of what's happening inside. Heart rate variability (HRV) offers a helpful window into your nervous system's state. It measures the small changes in time between each heartbeat.

When you're calm, and the vagus nerve is active, these intervals gently fluctuate. A flexible heart rhythm suggests that your body can recover from stress and adapt to challenges.

When stress or exhaustion becomes constant, those variations often shrink. The heart begins to beat with a more rigid pattern, which can signal that the nervous system is struggling to reset.

In simple terms, HRV reflects how flexible and resilient your nervous system is when facing the demands of daily life.

HRV tracking is now accessible without a doctor's visit or a trip to the lab. Fitness watches, chest straps, and rings, such as the Oura, as well as brands like Garmin and Polar, are known for their accurate HRV monitoring. However, simpler tools and apps can also provide valuable insights. Even free or affordable smartphone apps can use your camera or a basic sensor for tracking. Some apps include guided breathwork alongside real-time HRV feedback, making it simple for beginners.

Using HRV tools at home comes with both benefits and a few cautions. On the positive side, HRV provides concrete feedback, allowing you to see whether relaxation or self-care practices are helping, even on days when you might not feel much different. Tracking your numbers over time highlights patterns and shows which routines support better stress recovery or sleep.

Seeing progress measurably can also be motivating. It gives you a tangible reminder that your nervous system can adapt and strengthen with consistent care.

At the same time, it's important to approach HRV gently. If you tend to worry about health metrics or become fixated on numbers, treat HRV as a supportive guide rather than a score you must perfect. Many normal factors—such as illness, poor sleep, or heavy meals—can temporarily lower HRV.

For this reason, try to focus on long-term trends rather than daily fluctuations. If you have a heart rhythm condition or notice that tracking your body increases anxiety, talk with a healthcare provider before using HRV devices or apps.

A typical HRV biofeedback session is simple. Find a quiet space and sit for 5–10 minutes. Use your device as directed—keep your finger steady on a sensor, or fit the chest strap or smartwatch properly. Launch your app and start a session.

As you record your heartbeat, try slow breathing: inhale gently through your nose for about 4 seconds, then exhale slowly through slightly parted lips or with a quiet hum for 6 to 8 seconds. Most people see their HRV score rise after a few slow breaths, a sign of increased relaxation and vagal tone.

Don't treat HRV as a daily report card. Look for patterns instead of fixating on single-day dips due to poor sleep or extra stress—those are just signals, not failures. The actual value is in upward trends: maybe your average HRV improves over a couple of weeks, or you notice calmer recoveries after stress. Celebrate these small wins as encouragement, not as proof that you're "doing enough."

Some days your numbers will dip. Avoid letting the scores control your mood—if tracking adds stress, take a step back or only check weekly. Remember, HRV is just one tool among many. It can help redirect your self-care or explain changes in mood and sleep, but it's not the entire story. Learning to check in with your heart's rhythms can foster healthier, more flexible responses to life's demands, without self-judgment.

Interactive Element: Try Your First HRV Session

- Download a free HRV app (e.g., Elite HRV or Welltory)
- Sit quietly and attach or activate your device
- Relax for 2 minutes, eyes open or closed
- Inhale slowly for four counts, exhale gently for 6–8 counts
- Watch the live feedback as you breathe
- Log your feelings before and after; note any shifts in calmness or tension

Let exploration, not perfectionism, guide you here. Approach HRV practice with curiosity and self-kindness—it's a tool for noticing and nurturing your nervous system's response to care.

Mindful Body Scanning and Sensory Awareness

Body scanning may sound simple—just noticing sensations from head to toe—but for those weighed down by anxiety, trauma, or chronic health issues, it can be a game-changer. It's not some mystical practice. Instead, it offers a practical way to awaken your body's internal "radar," which science calls interoception.

When you feel numb, disconnected, or out of touch, these exercises can gently help you reconnect and get back online. They strengthen vagal pathways by focusing attention on raw sensation, nudging your nervous system toward presence and safety, even when stress or pain wants to pull you in the opposite direction.

The guided practice begins. Choose a position that feels natural—whether sitting or lying down—so your body can relax without strain.

Bring your attention to the top of your head. Notice—without judgment—any tingling, warmth, or even blankness there. Move slowly down to your forehead, eyebrows, and eyes. Pause and sense whatever is present: a twitch, heaviness, or tension. If nothing appears, that's fine—"blank" is still a signal.

Continue moving down through your face and jaw. Notice your neck and shoulders, then scan down through your arms, hands, and each finger.

Bring your focus to your chest and feel your breath moving in and out. Let your attention drift downward through your ribs, belly, back, and hips, pausing wherever you notice sensation—or even neutrality.

Continue the gentle scan through your thighs, knees, calves, ankles, feet, and toes. At each point, simply notice: is there warmth, coolness, tingling, pulsing, pain, or nothing at all?

Breathe slowly. If your focus drifts away, gently return to the last place you remember.

Science offers a helpful explanation for why this works. When you focus on body sensations in real time, you activate parts of the sensory cortex and the insular cortex—areas of the brain that process signals from the skin, muscles, and internal organs.

This kind of attention can quiet the brain's alarm system, which constantly scans for threats or reacts to old emotional patterns. That's one reason body scanning can calm stress responses.

For people who often feel numb or dissociated—sometimes as a protective response to trauma—these scans can help rebuild the connection between mind and body. They gently reintroduce a sense of safe awareness.

The goal isn't to force dramatic sensations. It's simply to notice what is already there.

Sensory awareness doesn't stop with scanning. There are many ways to explore sensation if focusing inward feels uncomfortable or unfamiliar. Try texture exploration: rub two different fabrics between your fingers—perhaps a soft blanket and denim or corduroy—and notice the difference in roughness or warmth.

You can also use weighted objects for grounding. Hold a small bean bag or a filled water bottle in your lap and notice its weight pressing gently downward. Temperature can offer another doorway into sensation. Soak your hands in warm water for a minute or press a cool compress against your cheeks and observe how your body responds.

Scent immersion can also be surprisingly effective. Smell a drop of lavender oil, coffee grounds, or even the pages of an old book, and notice how your body reacts. Some scents may energize you, while others encourage relaxation.

Not everyone feels comfortable closing their eyes or focusing inward, especially if past trauma lives in the body or certain areas hold painful memories. That response is normal and valid.

You can always adapt the practice. If focusing on the chest brings up anxiety or sadness, skip it or move on quickly.

An "outside-in" approach can feel safer for some people. Keep your eyes open and name five things you see in the room before turning attention inward. You might alternate between noticing an object—such as a lamp or pillow—and sensing your hand resting on your leg or the floor beneath your feet.

This gentle back-and-forth can help keep you grounded if the body scan becomes overwhelming.

Interactive Element: Sensory Awareness Menu

- **Texture:** Rub two fabrics (try soft and rough) and notice the temperature differences. Squeeze a small ball.
- **Weight:** Hold a weighted object in your lap; let it ground and relax you.
- **Temperature:** Place your hands in warm water for 30 seconds, then switch to cool water for contrast.
- **Scent:** Smell something familiar (herbs, tea leaves) with full attention.

- **Visual:** Trace the outline of an object with your eyes while noticing any shifts inside.

If one area of your body feels uncomfortable—say your stomach after eating or your jaw when anxious—either skip it or "touch and go," checking in briefly before moving on. There is no right way to do this; what matters is your sense of control and comfort. Over time, these practices build trust with your body and offer new ways to calm a restless mind without shutting down or checking out.

Safe Embodiment Practices for Trauma Survivors

If you're carrying the aftershocks of trauma, the idea of returning to your body can feel almost impossible. After what you've lived through, your body might not feel like home. You may notice numbness, a sense of floating outside yourself, or waves of fear or disgust when you try to check in with physical sensations.

On some days, even a small internal shift—like your heart racing or your stomach tightening—can set off an alarm in your system. These responses show that your nervous system is trying to protect you, not that you've failed or that something is wrong. They are survival strategies your body developed to keep you safe during overwhelming moments.

Because of that, the real challenge isn't simply learning techniques. It's slowly rebuilding trust with your body, at a pace that feels safe for you.

Reconnecting after trauma often requires a gentler rhythm. Instead of diving in all at once, imagine dipping a toe into cold water. A helpful approach is called titration. Titration involves allowing yourself very small doses of sensation.

You might check in for only a second or two—perhaps noticing the feeling of your hand resting on your leg or the pressure of your feet against the floor—before shifting your attention back to something neutral.

Another helpful tool is pendulation. Pendulation involves gently moving your focus between a neutral or comfortable area and one that feels more charged.

For example, place one hand on your chest and the other on your thigh. You might notice warmth in your thigh and tension in your chest. Stay with the warmth for a few moments, then briefly notice the chest before returning your attention to the thigh.

This slow back-and-forth helps your nervous system process sensations without becoming overwhelmed.

Having support nearby can also make a big difference. You don't have to face these sensations alone. The presence of a trusted friend, therapist, or even a calm pet can provide the sense of safety your nervous system needs.

This process is often called co-regulation—when your nervous system steadies itself through contact with another regulated being.

If activation begins to rise—tight chest, dizziness, tears—having a simple rescue plan can help. Your plan might include stepping outside to call someone you trust, sending a quick text to a friend, or holding something comforting.

Some people keep a weighted blanket nearby. Others calm themselves by naming five things they can see or hear around them.

The goal is never to force yourself through distress. The goal is to recognize the signal, honor it, and guide yourself back toward safety whenever you need to.

Building trust with your body can take weeks, months, or even longer. There's no proper timeline here, and every small step counts. Maybe one day you notice the soft texture of your shirt against your skin for half a second before dissociation tugs you away. Another day, you realize you've been breathing more deeply without thinking about it. Don't dismiss these moments—they are signs that your body is willing to let you back in, even briefly.

You can reinforce safety by integrating supportive rituals before and after any embodiment work. Light a candle, wrap up in something soft, play a calming song, or set an intention ("I will only do what feels safe today"). If sitting still isn't possible, try gentle movements, such as tapping your fingers or rocking side to side. Walking while noticing the sensation of your feet on the ground can be just as effective as formal practices.

Tracking progress helps, too. After any practice, pause and ask yourself: "What did I notice in my body today, even if it lasted just a second?" Or jot down this reflection: "Was there a moment when I felt safe or at least neutral?" Some survivors find it helpful to keep a journal or voice memo log—just a sentence or two describing anything new they discovered about their body's reactions. This record becomes evidence that change is happening, even if it feels slow.

Trauma survivors often feel shame when progress seems small or inconsistent. That reaction is entirely normal—healing rarely progresses in a straight line. Celebrate every tiny spark of presence as a real achievement. If all you can do is recognize that you're holding your breath and then sigh once, that's enough for today. Over time, these micro-moments add up, building bridges back to yourself.

Remember: You are not alone in this work, and no one expects perfection from you—not me, not anyone worth trusting. If embodiment ever feels overwhelming, give yourself permission to pause and ground. Return when you're ready, or reach out for help if things get sticky. Your body has always been trying to protect you; now it deserves gentleness as you learn to listen again.

"Resilience Stacks": Layering Techniques for Maximal Benefit

When life overwhelms you, it's common to feel as if the simple tools you've learned—like breathing exercises or humming—offer only fleeting relief.

What often gets overlooked is the amplifying effect of combining several simple practices into a sequence—a concept known as "resilience stacking." Think of it as curating a playlist for your well-being, where each technique enhances the next. The goal isn't to complicate your day, but rather to amplify the impact of your current self-care and to improve adaptability, especially when symptoms shift rapidly.

Layering works because your nervous system responds to repeated, varied signals of safety. While a single tool can help, combining two or three in succession creates a reinforcing effect. Pairing breathwork, grounding, and gentle vagus nerve stimulation sends multiple "safe" messages to your body. Together, these practices support bigger changes.

Breathing can slow your heart rate, humming can create a gentle vibration in your chest and throat, self-massage can ease tension, and grounding thoughts can steady your mind. Together, these don't just add up—they multiply each other's benefits, making resilience more accessible even during challenging times.

Different scenarios call for other stacks. If mornings are difficult, try this simple routine before leaving bed: pause to find one thing you're grateful for (even if it's just your pillow), hum softly for a minute or two, then do a few gentle movements like shoulder rolls or stretches. This trio gently wakes your body and nervous system, setting a foundation of calm energy rather than defaulting to stress.

For acute stress or sudden spikes in anxiety or pain, an "emergency stack" can quickly break the cycle. Splash cold water on your face or wrists to signal your vagus nerve to calm down. Follow with slow, exhale-focused breaths (such as pursed-lip or straw breathing), and end with a minute of gentle massage on your ears or jaw areas, where anxiety commonly lingers. These steps are swift and require no special tools, making them ideal for quick breaks at work or elsewhere.

Evenings have their challenges. If winding down is tough and sleep is elusive, try stacking sensory grounding (hold a weighted object or wrap up in a soft blanket), a brief body scan (notice your breath), and three long, slow exhales. This stack soothes nerves and helps the mind shift from alertness toward rest.

Creating your stack is straightforward—tune in to how you feel and identify your loudest symptoms. Are you anxious, numb, in pain, or stuck in worry? Let the earlier symptom tracking guide you. Start with a technique that feels manageable—perhaps humming for anxiety or grounding touch for dissociation. Add a second and third practice that addresses your needs. On low-energy days, keep it minimal—just gratitude and humming. On better days, layer in gentle movement or a quick cold splash.

A simple template:

1. Choose an anchor (gratitude, intention, grounding thought).
2. Pick a physical technique (breathing, humming, or cold splash).
3. Finish with sensory or touch-based practice (self-massage, texture exploration).

Switching up stacks prevents routines from becoming stale. Try changing the order or adding new practices each week to keep your routine fresh and engaging. Some people like listing their favorite stacks on note cards or their phone for easy access, especially during periods of brain fog or flare-ups.

Experiment—there's no perfect stack, and your needs will change. If something isn't working or feels overwhelming, simplify or adjust. Flexibility and self-compassion matter most—affirm to yourself: "My routine can change as often as I do." Each attempt builds resilience.

If you're in a support group or have friends on a similar journey, consider sharing and discussing stacks. Hearing others' routines can spark new ideas or validate your practices.

As this chapter on advanced vagus nerve techniques ends, remember: resilience is not about rigid routines, but having a variety of options and knowing how to layer them when challenges arise. Stacking small tools creates bigger outcomes, making self-care more effective, adaptable, and personal to you.

Next, we'll explore integrating vagus nerve work with other wellness practices, including nutrition, movement, and rest, to cultivate lasting balance throughout all aspects of daily life.

Chapter 9

Support, Setbacks, and Long-Term Success

What to Do When Symptoms Return: The "Bounce-Back Plan"

Feeling discouraged when old symptoms come back is normal, especially after making progress. You might experience a sudden return of anxiety, chest tightness, digestive upset, or insomnia, leading you to worry you're back at square one. But setbacks aren't failures—they're part of the healing process. Recovery isn't linear; the nervous system learns and adapts in cycles, so ups and downs are a natural part of the process. Your nervous system responds with setbacks as it works to relearn what safety feels like.

When symptoms return, your mind might default to negative self-talk—"I knew this wouldn't last," or "I'll never get better." It's important to recognize this as part of the process, especially if you're undoing deep-rooted patterns from trauma, chronic illness, or stress. Feeling frustrated, sad, or angry is a valid experience; let those emotions come without harsh self-judgment.

Your first bounce-back step is to interrupt the story in your mind that says you've failed. When symptoms return, pause and tell yourself out loud:

"This is a setback, not a failure." Hearing those words can stop the spiral of self-criticism. Instead of trying to fix everything at once, choose one small practice to help settle your system. You might try a slow exhale with your hand on your chest, a gentle hum, or splashing cool water on your face. Focus on one calming action, not a whole routine. Treat that small step as a quick reset, a way to signal safety to your body.

After your micro-practice, take a moment to ground yourself before returning to your daily routines.

Grounding can be simple: place both feet on the floor, name three things you see, play calming music, or wrap yourself in a favorite blanket—whatever helps your body feel stable and safe enough to try again. This kind of self-support is more vital in the moment than any perfect routine.

When you've stabilized, it's helpful to review your symptom logs or notes, if you keep them, but do this with curiosity, not blame.

Look for recent disruptions: Was there a sleepover? Did you skip meals? Was stress higher? Perhaps you broke your routines, had a big deadline, received bad news, traveled, or had an argument with someone. Sometimes triggers are clear; other times, even small changes—such as disrupted sleep or hydration—can spark symptoms. Rather than over-analyzing, scan for broad patterns.

If you spot something—like stopping breathwork or eating late—note it as helpful feedback rather than ammunition against yourself: "I stopped breathwork when work was busy," or "Late dinners led to more gut flares." Let these patterns guide you to reintroduce helpful habits one by one, gently. If the trigger isn't apparent, that's normal, too. Bodies are complex, and randomness is an inherent part of the cycle.

Set realistic expectations after a setback. It's tempting to want instant recovery, but healing from anxiety, chronic pain, trauma, or gut issues is gradual. Instead of all-or-nothing thinking, focus on small wins: Maybe the anxiety didn't last as long as before, or sleep bounced back after a couple of rough nights. Even a faster recovery is progress worth noting.

Journaling is helpful here—try prompts like "What helped last time?" or "What small shift did I notice?" Write down what grounded you—a walk, a conversation, a breathing practice—or what let you know you were improving, like less pain in the morning or easier digestion after dinner. Celebrating minor improvements helps your mind focus on progress rather than just setbacks.

Interactive Element: Your Bounce-Back Checklist

Create your bounce-back checklist and keep it handy—on your phone, journal, or somewhere visible:

Bounce-Back Checklist

1. Pause and say: "This is a setback, not a reversal."

2. Choose ONE micro-practice:

- Slowly exhale with hand on heart
- Humming or soft singing
- Splash cool water on your face
- Sensory grounding (notice feet on floor, touch an object)
- Gentle neck/ear massage

1. Ground yourself before restarting your routines (try using music, a blanket, or nature sounds).
2. Review the symptom log and notes for recent changes or triggers.
3. Journal: "What did I do last time that helped?"
4. Celebrate any small win (faster recovery, less symptom intensity).
5. Remind yourself: progress comes in cycles, not perfection.

Setbacks will come, but using this checklist helps you move from frustration to gentle action and renewed hope.

Each time you walk through this process, you teach your nervous system it's safe to return to calm, even after hard days. Over time, these cycles usually get shorter and less intense. You'll start to trust that—even if anxiety or gut symptoms flare up—you have practical tools for recovery.

If you find yourself stuck in a setback for longer than usual, remember this doesn't mean all is lost. Sometimes bodies need a little more time, or outside stresses are higher. The fact that you continue to show up for yourself, regardless of what the symptom chart indicates, is significant. Healing isn't about avoiding every storm; it's about knowing how to find steadiness and safety when rough waves come again.

Building a Support System: Community, Accountability, and Safe Sharing

Healing can feel overwhelming when you try to do it alone. Persistent symptoms like anxiety, fatigue, gut pain, or insomnia often seem more complicated to carry in isolation, and motivation tends to fade when challenges arise.

Even a small connection with someone who understands can lighten the load and help you see your struggles as shared rather than personal failings. It takes courage to reach out, especially if you're used to guarding your pain or have experienced broken trust, but healing alongside others often brings comfort that solitude cannot.

You don't need a large group or to bare your soul to everyone. Sometimes, support starts with just one person-a friend, a relative, or even an understanding online contact—who listens without judgment.

If you don't have someone like that in your current circle, consider seeking out groups focused on nervous system health or holistic wellness. Many such communities exist online, from moderated Facebook groups and healing forums to meetups posted on community boards or libraries.

These spaces lift you. They cheer you on when things feel heavy. They pass along ideas that work in real life—not just theories—and they remind you, in quiet but powerful ways, that you're not doing this alone. When you step into a shared space—a meditation circle or a local support group—you feel it. There's an unspoken sense of "we're in this together." It's the kind of connection that can soften the loneliness and help you breathe a little easier.

It's easier to stick with healing routines when you have support. Find a "calm buddy"—someone you trust enough to check in with regularly. Not to push or judge, but to gently remind you that progress is still progress, and setbacks are part of the journey. Maybe you send each other a quick text after trying a new vagus nerve exercise, or just a kind word on a hard day.

You don't need to check in every single day. Just a message once or twice a week—a simple "How are you holding up?" or "I tried that exercise today"—can go a long way. It's enough to feel like someone's in your corner, that you're not carrying everything alone.

If jumping into a group feels like too much, it's okay to ease in slowly. Start by simply observing. Read a few posts—notice who seems kind, who shares honestly, and who makes you feel safe. Follow the voices that feel gentle and encouraging.

You don't have to speak right away—sometimes, just being there is enough to feel a little less alone. When you're ready, introduce yourself as much or as little as comfortable—sometimes a simple, "I'm working on my sleep and looking for new habits," is all it takes to receive encouragement and advice.

Over time, these small exchanges foster trust and lead to deeper friendships or in-person meetings.

When sharing within a group or with an individual, consider what you're comfortable revealing. Trust develops gradually, particularly if trauma makes sharing feel risky. Decide beforehand what feels okay—maybe just mentioning sleep struggles or workplace anxiety. You're never obligated to share your medical history or deep pain unless you choose to. Please start with the boundaries that keep you feeling safe, and expand them as trust allows. Remember, people have their perspectives and limitations—someone's inability to relate doesn't mean your experience is any less valid.

Supportive listening sustains healing relationships. Whether you're sharing or listening, focus on curiosity and compassion rather than trying to solve the problem. Often, simply hearing "That sounds hard" or "I see your effort" can be more helpful than advice.

If you need something specific—such as encouragement after a setback or support in sticking to routines—state your needs directly. For instance: "Could I text you when I feel panicky?" or "Would you check in after my first week of new exercises?" Clear requests make it easier for others to support you and help establish healthy boundaries.

If you're unsure how to ask for help, here are some example scripts:

- "I'm trying something new for my anxiety and would love a buddy to talk to every few days—would you be open to that?"
- "Sometimes I just need a listening ear when I'm frustrated—no advice needed."
- "On hard days with my gut symptoms, can I send you a quick update? Encouragement really helps."
- "Can we celebrate my wins together? Even the small ones matter to me."

Celebrating even the tiniest wins together helps you see just how far you've come—and reminds you that progress isn't always loud or big.

Sharing one good thing every Friday is a simple weekly ritual that can quietly weave a group together. Maybe someone says, "I took a deep breath before that tough conversation," or "I actually got a decent night's sleep." These moments might seem small, but they're not. They're reminders that healing is happening, even in the little things. And when you share them, it helps everyone feel seen, encouraged, and not so alone.

These check-ins aren't about comparing or trying to do more than someone else—they're about showing up for each other, noticing the effort, and saying, "I see you. You're doing great."

On tough days, communal support eases the sting of setbacks. Buddy check-ins after flare-ups remind you that others have faced similar struggles and have recovered. Community challenges, such as a "7-Day Micro-Calm Streak," where everyone tries a vagus nerve practice daily and reports back, foster connection and keep accountability gentle and supportive.

For those new to safe sharing, boundaries are crucial. If something feels off or a person crosses a line, it's okay to step back. Select healing communities that genuinely uphold respect, privacy, and non-judgmental guidelines.

A support system isn't about fixing each other but creating space for growth and setbacks alike. Healing together means celebrating courage—whether it's starting a new routine, surviving a hard week, or simply showing up when disappearing would be easier. The relationships you nurture may not erase pain instantly, but they offer steady support when things feel uncertain.

Sometimes, simply seeing a familiar name in your messages is enough to remind you that healing doesn't have to be lonely. With rituals, gentle accountability, and open conversation, community transforms personal struggle into collective hope—a hope that grows stronger every time someone says, "Me too," or "I'm still here."

Navigating Medical Care: Talking to Your Doctor About Vagus Nerve Practice

Discussing your health practices—especially those that are less conventional—with a doctor or therapist can be stressful. Many fear their provider will dismiss their efforts or be skeptical of anything "alternative." Still, being open about your vagus nerve practices can meaningfully improve your care and, sometimes, even strengthen your partnership with your healthcare team.

Being transparent matters. If you're dealing with anxiety, trauma, chronic inflammation, gut problems, or sleep issues, your doctor needs the whole picture.

Telling them about new techniques—such as breathing, humming, or self-massage—shows you're proactive and helps them account for potential interactions with your medications or treatments. It also helps ensure your care is safer, as your doctor can monitor for side effects or conflicts and make adjustments if necessary.

Initiating this conversation can feel awkward, especially if you haven't discussed mind-body practices before. Preparing a few simple sentences can help.

For example: "I'm doing some vagus nerve exercises—breathing, humming, gentle cold exposure—for anxiety and gut issues. They help, and I want to be sure they're safe with my treatment plan." Or: "I learned about vagus nerve stimulation for chronic stress and inflammation. I'm continuing these exercises with my current plan." These kinds of statements make it clear you value your doctor's guidance but are committed to your well-being.

At your appointment, ask open, inviting questions, such as: "Is there any risk using these techniques with my current medications or diagnoses?" or "Any reason I should avoid these exercises?" Asking questions like these lets your provider know you value their knowledge and welcome their guidance.

If you also see a therapist or psychiatrist, be sure to mention your somatic practices during those visits as well. Many therapists already use grounding and breathwork techniques, and others may be open to learning from your experience.

If your provider responds with skepticism, try to stay calm. Not all providers are familiar with recent research on the nervous system or polyvagal theory.

If you can, bring a short study summary or a reputable article: "I've found some information about these techniques—would you be open to looking at it?" Or share your symptom logs: "Since starting these exercises, I've had less pain/better sleep (show data)." Objective information often shifts the conversation from "I read this online" to "Here's what's changed for me." If your provider seems hurried, offer to leave the material for later review and consideration.

If you encounter a complete lack of openness, try to maintain a constructive approach. Ask about a "let's try and monitor" plan: "Would you be willing to watch my symptoms with me as I continue these practices over the next few months?" Turning the situation into a partnership usually works better than confrontation.

Those with trauma histories or chronic illnesses may find it especially helpful to seek out integrative or trauma-informed providers. These professionals are more likely to blend conventional and mind-body approaches.

When searching, use terms like "integrative medicine," "functional medicine," "trauma-informed care," or "mind-body specialist," and consult patient communities for recommendations about providers that listen and support self-healing.

When meeting new providers, treat it like an interview. Ask questions such as: "How do you feel about patients doing mind-body techniques at home?" or "Are you open to discussing how stress and trauma affect health?"

Please pay attention to their listening skills, curiosity, and willingness to learn alongside you. Their openness is often more valuable than having all the answers.

Sometimes you'll need to explain the basics. Brief, simple explanations—"The vagus nerve regulates stress, digestion, and inflammation; these exercises help tone that system"—can bridge knowledge gaps without overwhelming providers.

If your doctor asks for more details, describe the changes you've noticed: "Slow breathing and humming before meals reduced my stomach pain," or "Since adding self-massage at bedtime, I'm sleeping deeper."

If your provider expresses safety concerns, reassure them that these are gentle practices. Offer to keep a symptom log, and invite collaboration: "If anything worsens or changes, I'll let you know right away." This approach demonstrates that you're not disregarding their advice but are thoughtfully integrating different strategies.

If you ever feel dismissed or not listened to, remember your lived experience counts. It's reasonable to seek out practitioners who value your input and support experimentation within safe limits. A supportive care team will celebrate your progress and respect your perspective as valid.

The most empowered patients often arrive prepared, with questions, curiosity, and self-advocacy, rather than arguments. You have the right to ask about recommendations, bring your research, and expect collaboration rather than just direction from your care team. Healing is a partnership: providers have expertise, but you bring insight into your body—both are crucial.

Navigating healthcare with practices outside the mainstream can be challenging. But every honest conversation you start creates a foundation for care that fits your needs, not just what's standard or prescribed.

Adapting to Life Changes: Routines for Travel, Work, and Family Stress

Life is constantly shifting—routines get disrupted by travel, work deadlines, family chaos, or even joyful events like vacations. Being out of your comfort zone, sleeping in new places, eating unusual foods, or just feeling depleted can quickly unsettle nervous system practices and open the door to anxiety, gut issues, or sleep trouble. But adaptation, not rigid routine, is the real key to staying calm and well in any scenario.

Portable Practices for On-the-Go Calm

When you're on the move or under pressure, you need practices you can do anywhere. Humming under your breath during tense moments—at the airport, in a waiting room, or whenever you feel nervous—can help. A gentle massage behind your ear or at your jaw can offer calm and signal your vagus nerve to reset. Cold water is also adequate; whether on a road trip or layover, splashing your face or holding a cold bottle to your neck can quickly soothe your nerves.

Travel Tips for Nervous System Support

Travel often presents challenges such as restlessness and disrupted sleep. Try breathwork in your seat—slow, nasal inhales, long, relaxed exhales through pursed lips. If you're uncomfortable doing deep breathing openly, use sensory grounding: press your feet into the floor, touch textured clothing, or hold a smooth stone in your pocket. These anchor you in the present, no equipment needed.

Hotel rooms or unfamiliar spaces can unsettle sleep or digestion. Creating a mini safe zone helps: toss calming essential oil or an eye mask in your bag, and bring a playlist of soothing sounds from home. These small comforts transform any space into a personal retreat. For trouble sleeping, try slow breathing or gentle humming while in bed—forget about forcing a perfect sleep ritual.

Handling Family Stress and Social Events

Family gatherings or social events can bring unique stress from noise or out-of-sync routines. Take quick bathroom breaks for micro-resets—try deep breathing, humming, or sipping cold water to refresh yourself. Stepping outside for a moment, noticing the breeze or the ground beneath you, can reset your system and alleviate feelings of overwhelm.

Calming Work Stress

Work often feels overwhelming, especially when you're facing long meetings or pressure to meet tight deadlines. Desk-based micro-practices help: slow breathing with a hand on your belly while checking emails, gentle jaw-ear massage during calls, or slow sips of cold water as a ritual.

In more public or formal settings, you can try subtle techniques such as gently pressing your tongue to the top of your mouth while exhaling, tracing the edge of your desk with your finger, or resting your gaze on something soothing.

Embracing Imperfect Routines

Sometimes, routines unravel, and all you manage is a single slow breath or a minute of humming. That small action isn't a failure—it's a sign of healthy flexibility. Adapting in the moment shows you're listening to your needs and doing what you can, rather than chasing perfection. Give yourself permission to pause, scale back, or miss a routine without guilt. Self-forgiveness is as important as any physical practice for nervous system health.

Planning for Transitions

Planning can make transitions smoother. For trips or busy weeks, pack a small "nervous system kit"—your favorite essential oil, eye mask, earplugs, an offline playlist, a comforting scarf, a water bottle that doubles as a cold compress, and a grounding stone or stress ball. For stressful work or family days, set brief reminders on your phone ("Exhale slowly," "Hum for one minute," "Massage jaw"). Sometimes, ask a friend or partner for a check-in message if you need one.

Create your portable toolkit: herbal tea bags, a favorite photo, scented lotion, or a list of contacts for encouragement. Before traveling or during busy weeks, quickly jot down the likely stressors and basic calming rituals you can slip in when needed. Don't aim for perfection—aim for calm.

Practicing Self-Compassion

If you forget your tools or routines fall away completely during chaos, be gentle with yourself. Skip the blame—every day offers a chance to reset. Your nervous system responds to kindness and repetition, not punishment.

Flexibility as Your Superpower

Adaptability is vital during life's unpredictable seasons. These tiny moments of calm—scattered among travel, family events, and busy workdays—add up. They keep your vagus nerve responsive, even when everything else feels shaky.

As you practice these skills, maintaining calm amid disruption gets easier. Each adaptation you make strengthens the foundation for deeper, lasting wellness.

Genuine healing requires flexibility as you navigate life's changes. You don't need to be perfect—consistent engagement matters more than a flawless routine. Next, we'll explore how to deepen mind-body wellness in ways that fit into everyday life.

Chapter 10

Beyond the Basics: Integrating Vagus Nerve Work with Holistic Wellness

Nutrition and the Vagus Nerve: Foods That Support Nervous System Healing

If you've ever felt your mood crash after junk food or experienced stress that caused stomach issues, you've seen the gut-brain connection in action. What you eat doesn't just impact your waistline or lab results—it shapes your daily resilience, energy, and sense of calm. For those facing anxiety, trauma, gut issues, or poor sleep, food can feel both overwhelming and essential.

In practice, you may wonder whether a single meal choice matters when everything else feels stuck. The answer is yes: nutrition isn't about rigid rules or perfect diets—it's about consistently supporting your nervous system in simple, manageable ways.

Nutrition's link to the vagus nerve is a two-way street. The vagus nerve relays signals between your brain and gut, interpreting hunger, fullness, and discomfort. Notably, about 80% of these signals travel from the body to the brain, meaning your gut's state influences your mood, thoughts, and sense of safety

Intestinal inflammation from processed foods or sensitivities doesn't stay in your gut; the vagus nerve senses the turmoil and can contribute to anxiety or irritability. Choosing foods that soothe your gut can calm your mind, ease pain, and improve sleep.

Blood sugar swings often drive nervous system unrest. Breakfasts high in refined carbs or sugary drinks can quickly raise and then drop your blood sugar levels, leading to shifts in mood and energy that may fuel anxiety.

Stable blood sugar is a gift to your vagus nerve, helping your body stay out of "emergency mode" and encouraging calm. Minor tweaks—such as adding protein or healthy fats to breakfast (e.g., eggs with avocado, oats with walnuts)—help slow sugar absorption and stabilize energy levels.

Specific nutrients can boost vagal tone and reduce inflammation. You'll find omega-3 fatty acids in foods like salmon, sardines, flaxseeds, chia seeds, and walnuts—they help reduce inflammation and support healthy nerve function.

For those who avoid fish, sprinkling ground flaxseed on oats or snacking on walnuts is a simple swap. Polyphenols—found in berries, leafy greens, and dark chocolate—act as antioxidants, fighting inflammation and nourishing both gut bacteria and the nervous system. Instead of a candy bar, try a few squares of dark chocolate (70% cocoa or higher) with berries to satisfy a sweet craving while supporting calm.

Fermented foods are powerful allies for the gut-brain axis. Some foods, such as yogurt with live cultures, kefir, kimchi, sauerkraut, miso, and kombucha, contain beneficial bacteria that interact with the vagus nerve through chemical signaling.

These microbes lower inflammation and produce neurotransmitters, especially serotonin, which the gut makes in large amounts. New to fermented foods? Start small: a spoonful of sauerkraut with lunch or a few sips of kefir at breakfast.

Keeping this simple is key. The goal isn't to overhaul your diet overnight, but to make manageable changes that add up over time.

Practical strategies: toss berries into cereal or yogurt in the morning; add spinach or kale to soups, smoothies, or omelets; keep walnuts on hand for snacks; replace chips with roasted chickpeas or carrots with hummus. If meal prep or food costs are obstacles, know that frozen berries and greens work just as well as fresh and are often more affordable.

Interactive Element: Quick-Start Gut-Brain Food Checklist

- Add a tablespoon of ground chia seeds or flaxseed to your oatmeal, smoothie, or salad for a nutritious boost.
- Top toast or porridge with avocado or walnuts.
- Include berries (fresh or frozen) in breakfast or snacks.
- Top your sandwich or grain bowl with a spoonful of sauerkraut or kimchi.
- Swap soda for unsweetened iced green tea.

- Choose dark leafy greens (spinach, kale) for salads or cooked sides.
- Pair your tea with a few pieces of dark chocolate that's at least 70% cocoa.

Some foods don't support vagal health. Highly processed snacks with artificial ingredients or trans fats can irritate the gut and inflame the nervous system. Excessive caffeine provides short-lived energy but may leave you feeling jittery and anxious. Unless these foods noticeably trigger you, it's not about strict elimination, but about noting how you feel and making gradual improvements.

Another overlooked tool is mindful eating. Sitting down, chewing thoroughly, and eating in a calm space can dramatically improve digestion and vagal signaling. Try pausing between bites, taking a few deep breaths before meals, or simply paying attention to the textures and flavors of your food. Mindful eating isn't about guilt or discipline—it's about sending safety cues to your body so it can relax and absorb nutrients more effectively.

If changing your food habits feels overwhelming, or if emotional eating is a familiar pattern, start with just one shift—maybe a different snack this week or trying fermented foods once. Celebrate every incremental change, since each supports digestion, mood, energy, and sleep. Some days, convenience will win, and that's okay. The important thing is building small patterns that collectively encourage healing.

If restrictive diets have burned you before, treat this approach as an experiment, not a punishment. The aim isn't perfection but reconnecting with what nourishes you, not just what matches an ideal.

Food is more than fuel—it's communication between gut, brain, body, and mind. Every meal presents an opportunity to support your nervous system, even on challenging days, in a subtle yet effective way. Over time, these small shifts become acts of self-respect, helping you feel sturdier and more resilient from the inside out.

Emotional Processing and Journaling for Deeper Calm

Stress and anxiety aren't always loud or obvious; sometimes they linger quietly in the body for days or years. When emotions remain unprocessed—such as anger, grief, fear, or shame—they can keep your nervous system in a heightened state, making it harder to unwind, rest, or feel at ease in your body.

Many people focus on physical recovery but struggle to make progress when they ignore their emotional well-being. Your vagus nerve helps regulate relaxation and reacts to both how you move your body and what you feel emotionally. Emotional awareness and gentle self-expression foster a more profound, lasting calm from the inside out.

Emotions aren't just intangible feelings—they create real physical signals: tight throats, churning stomachs, a heaviness in the chest. When you suppress these signals, they can intensify over time, triggering migraines, flare-ups, or panic attacks. Even small, unprocessed moments like last week's argument or long-held grief can shape your body's stress response. Rather than avoiding these emotions, gently turning toward them—however intimidating it may seem at first—can help release their hold. Small, structured steps make this process manageable and even comforting.

One powerful tool is structured journaling, specifically "emotion-mapping." Take a blank page and note the times and places where you felt stress, anger, sadness, or physical tension each day. There's no need for perfection; honest, simple notes, such as "tight chest after that email" or "stomach in knots after talking to mom," are enough. Over time, patterns emerge—certain people or tasks repeatedly trigger stress. This awareness is the first step toward relief, illuminating where your nervous system gets stuck and needs support.

To make this practice easy, use daily prompts. At day's end, ask yourself questions like: "How did my body feel when I was stressed today?" "When did I feel safe or calm?" "Which emotion was strongest?" Write freely without worrying about anyone else reading. You don't need to fix anything—just notice. If whole sentences feel overwhelming, try jotting down single words or symbols instead. The key is connecting with what's happening inside.

Free writing is another simple technique to clear mental clutter. Set a five-minute timer and write without rules or self-editing—anything from complaints to random thoughts is fair game. Sometimes surprising insights appear: a forgotten memory, or a hidden anxiety. Releasing thoughts without judgment often softens the intensity of persistent emotions. Letter-writing can also help—write to yourself or to someone who hurt you, without any intention to send it. Pouring out these words allows your nervous system to release tension you may not realize you're holding.

If you struggle to put feelings into words, art can help. Express your emotions through colors and shapes—fiery red for anger, jagged yellow for anxiety, or heavy blue for sadness. Reflecting on your day while doodling can move stuck energy. There's no need for artistic skill; focus on expressing honestly, not making a masterpiece.

Incorporating quick emotional check-ins is easy—no lengthy routines or therapy sessions required. Small rituals, such as a brief "end-of-day reflection," can make a significant difference. Sit quietly for two minutes to notice which emotion showed up most and how you attempted to soothe it, even if you failed. Building this habit over time strengthens self-trust and self-compassion.

Some find it helpful to set up a "calm corner" at home—a cozy spot with soft light and comforting objects where you can retreat when overwhelmed. This space serves as a mini sanctuary for emotional self-care: somewhere to breathe, journal, cry, or sit quietly until you feel lighter.

If intense emotions arise during these practices, use grounding techniques to help you stay grounded. Feel your feet on the floor, notice the texture under your toes, splash cold water on your wrists, hold a cool object, or focus on distant sounds. These simple strategies can help you return to the present and regulate your nervous system.

There will be days when this work feels easier, and days you might avoid it—that's normal. Over time, you'll notice more space between stress and reaction, allowing your vagus nerve and your system to recover, rather than remain stuck.

If you encounter resistance—perhaps old messages that emotions are a weakness—pause and offer yourself understanding. Unlearning old habits takes patience. Remember, feeling deeply doesn't mean failing; it's a sign your system is ready to heal.

Steady practice—through emotion-mapping, journaling, art, and daily reflection—creates space for genuine, sustained calm and healing that physical practices alone can't achieve. Meeting emotions with compassion helps the nervous system heal—and the heart, too. This journey isn't about perfection; it's about discovering resilience, dignity, and the rest you deserve.

Building Your Personalized "Resilience Toolkit" for Lifelong Wellness

Living with anxiety, trauma, chronic inflammation, gut issues, or sleep struggles makes daily life unpredictable. Some mornings you feel steady; other days, a small trigger can throw you off. No single solution fits all, so building a flexible, personal "resilience toolkit" helps you navigate challenging times and strengthen your sense of calm. Creating your toolkit isn't about following generic advice—it's about discovering what truly soothes, grounds, and comforts you.

Start by recalling moments when you've felt a little steadier. Maybe it's wrapping up in a weighted blanket, using lavender oil, or holding a smooth stone. Physical items like these serve as anchors—simple reminders of your control, even during stressful times. Some find tension relief with an acupressure mat or ease nighttime worries with a heated neck wrap. While these tools won't erase symptoms, they interrupt negative spirals and give your nervous system a break.

Digital tools help too, especially in public spaces or busy homes. Meditation apps with brief guided sessions can reset you during a lunch break or before bed. Calming playlists for relaxation, focus, or sleep make it easy to shift your mood. HRV trackers can reveal how your body responds to different routines and stressors. Consider organizing your phone's folders with your favorite meditations, affirmations, and relaxing soundscapes for quick access.

Connection can also be part of your toolkit. If you've been managing symptoms on your own for a long time, reaching out may feel uncomfortable at first. But even one supportive person can help you stay consistent with your routines.

This might be someone who checks in after a hard week, a family member who reminds you to pause, or a therapist you can reach out to during moments of overwhelm. You might also keep a short list of support groups or resources—online or in person—that you can turn to when you need a reminder that you're not doing this alone.

Creative outlets bolster resilience. Art supplies—colored pencils, markers, sketchbooks—let you process feelings without words. Favorite books can comfort or help you make sense of your experience. Movement—such as stretching, walking, or dancing—breaks cycles of tension and worry, and sometimes just permitting yourself to do something enjoyable is as important as the activity itself.

Accessibility matters: don't let your toolkit gather dust in a drawer. Pack a pouch or box with key items like essential oil, earbuds, a mini journal, and something grounding (a stone or fidget toy). This way, you can reach for tools at work, while traveling, or at home. If digital tools work better for you, set up a dedicated note or folder on your phone for quick access to meditations, playlists, and essential contacts.

Checklists can clarify your options. List favorite breathing techniques (like box breathing or elongated exhale), grounding practices (splashing cool water, using a cold pack), and sensory comforts (a cozy blanket, peppermint tea). Include calming foods (bananas, herbal tea).

Whether you use three reliable tools or a dozen options, choose the one that best fits your needs.

Reflection keeps your toolkit relevant and helpful. Once a month, or anytime routines feel stale, ask yourself what's working and what's not. Maybe music helps at night, but not in the morning—swap out what's no longer useful and experiment with new ideas.

Reminders—via sticky notes or calendar alerts—can prompt you to check in regularly.

Let yourself experiment. One week might focus on nature walks and small, accessible practices, while another might concentrate on drawing while listening to rain sounds. Notice what genuinely helps you feel calmer, more present, or less tense.

If a tool stops being helpful or starts feeling like a chore, drop it—no guilt needed.

A good toolkit grows with you. Life changes: illnesses flare up, relationships shift, and work gets hectic—and your toolkit should adapt too. Treat it as an ongoing process of self-discovery, not something to perfect or "get right." Your needs will shift, and so should your supports.

During especially rough patches, try drawing from every category: one physical comfort (holding a favorite mug), one digital aid (music or meditation), one social contact (texting a friend), and one creative outlet (writing or doodling). Mix and match until something helps.

Wherever you are in this process—starting or refining routines—remember that small changes matter. Each tool in your collection is a testament to your choice of care and resilience, not resignation. It's not about having the "perfect" set, but about having options when things go sideways.

A physical box by your bed or a digital folder on your phone can feel like a lifeline. In moments of panic or exhaustion, simply seeing these items can remind you: you've weathered storms before, and you chose these tools because they genuinely help you.

Keep revisiting your toolkit. Check what's missing or what might help next time stress hits. Try a new scent, download a fresh playlist, join a different support group, or replace an old object with one that feels better now.

Your resilience toolkit is never static—it evolves alongside you. Over time, it grows from a box of helpful items into a symbol of self-trust and hope, promising that no matter what comes, you have ways to meet it with steadiness and care.

Resources, Further Reading, and Staying Motivated for the Journey

There comes a point where you want more—more understanding, more support, or just new voices whispering that you're not alone.

Sometimes you need fresh ideas, and at other times, you want a reminder that others have walked this path, stumbled, and persevered. No book can be the final word for your healing. That's why I'm sharing some of the best resources I've found—books that open eyes, podcasts that feel like wise friends, websites, and forums where real people swap stories and encouragement.

Bessel van der Kolk wrote a well-known book on trauma and healing, *The Body Keeps the Score*. If you're ready to explore further, consider starting there. It completely changed my understanding of the connection between the brain, the body, and the recovery process.

For those wrestling with exhaustion, *Burnout* by Emily and Amelia Nagoski is a lifeline. It explains why many of us get stuck in endless cycles of stress and offers practical ways to break free.

If you're curious about the science behind the vagus nerve and want a step-by-step approach, Stanley Rosenberg's book on vagus nerve healing offers a practical and approachable guide. Each of these books brings something different to the table: science, empathy, and real-world tools.

Podcasts can be powerful companions on hard days or during commutes. *The Huberman Lab*, with Dr. Andrew Huberman, breaks down neuroscience in a way that feels both smart and easy to follow. You'll find episodes on stress, sleep, brain health, and the nervous system's secrets.

The Doctor's Farmacy, with Dr. Mark Hyman, explores holistic health—covering everything from food to trauma to cutting-edge research—often featuring guests who share their own healing experiences.

Don't hesitate to scroll through their archives; sometimes an old episode is exactly what you need right now.

Online spaces can be challenging—filled with a lot of noise alongside valuable advice—but a few platforms stand out.

MindBodyGreen offers articles and community stories on topics such as gut health, anxiety relief, sleep, and more. The Polyvagal Institute's website (polyvagalinstitute.org) has accessible educational content on the vagus nerve and trauma recovery. Trusted forums like Reddit's r/Anxiety or r/ChronicIllness have active discussions where you can ask questions, vent, or read about what others are going through on their hardest days.

Sometimes what keeps us going is not information but inspiration—a sense that someone else has been where we are.

I think of Anna, who spent years cycling through panic attacks and IBS flares. She tried every new technique, hoping for a miracle. Nothing changed overnight. But she kept a simple log, celebrated tiny wins ("slept through the night," "ate dinner without pain"), and slowly noticed that her symptoms were changing—less severe, less frequent, and easier to recover from.

Or Sam, who felt numb for months after trauma but found comfort in short, daily movement routines and connecting online with others who understood dissociation. He credits his return to work and laughter not to one magic fix but to persistent small steps.

There's also power in community words. Readers often share encouragement like: "I thought I was broken—but now I see I was just overwhelmed," or "Progress felt invisible until I looked back at my notes and saw how far I'd come." These reminders aren't just fluff; they build self-trust when your own belief is shaky.

Staying motivated over months—or years—isn't about force of will. It's about creating reminders that your progress matters and that setbacks are not the end of the road. One method I suggest is setting quarterly intentions: every three months, write down a few gentle goals, such as "sleep through the night twice a week" or "try a new breathing practice." Review what worked and what didn't without blaming yourself. Make this reflection honest but kind—sometimes just noticing effort is enough.

Visual cues help, too. Some people make motivation boards with affirmations like "I am resilient," photos of loved ones, or sticky notes of small victories. If you're the digital type, keep pictures or voice memos on your phone for quick reference. Even better if you include reminders of times you got through a rough patch.

Accountability makes a difference for many. If you can, find a buddy—someone who checks in once a week, joins you in trying a new exercise, or even swaps texts about how it's going. Group check-ins work well too; some readers report that online challenges or support group routines help them stick with habits longer than going solo.

Above all else, bring curiosity to your self-care, not judgment. Your nervous system learns and adjusts all the time; it doesn't need perfection—it responds to steady, compassionate care. Allow your interests to shift over time: maybe one month podcasts help, another month it's art therapy or walks in nature. If you feel stuck or bored, revisit earlier chapters or try something completely new from the resources list.

You don't have to travel this road alone or in a straight line. There will be times when you want to quit, and days when you'll surprise yourself with how much strength you find. Every resource—book, podcast, community—exists to remind you that healing isn't about reaching an endpoint but about discovering tools that help you feel more like yourself.

Healing your nervous system is not about perfection. It is about learning to listen to your body again.

Every breath you slow, every moment you pause, and every small practice you repeat teaches your nervous system something powerful: that safety is possible again.

Change rarely happens overnight, but with patience and practice, your body can relearn calm. The tools in this book are not meant to be used once and forgotten—they are practices you can return to whenever life starts to feel overwhelming.

Your nervous system has been protecting you for years. Now it is time to help it heal.

Conclusion

If you're still with me, I want to take a moment to recognize how far you've come. Reading this book, trying even one new thing, or just being open to the idea of change—that's real courage. I know how easy it is to feel stuck, overwhelmed, or even hopeless when anxiety, trauma, gut struggles, or restless nights have been your norm for so long. I hope that as you close these pages, you see your nervous system—and yourself—with a little more compassion and trust.

The purpose of this book has always been straightforward: to restore your sense of control and hope.

By learning about the vagus nerve and practicing these science-backed exercises, you now have tools to help ease anxiety, support emotional healing, lower inflammation, soothe your gut, and improve your sleep. And you don't need fancy gadgets, a medical degree, or hours of spare time. You need curiosity, a willingness to try, and the reminder that healing is possible for you, regardless of your past, diagnosis, or starting point.

Let's quickly look back at the path we've traveled together. You began by meeting the vagus nerve—your body's own "reset button"—and learning why it matters for everything from mood to digestion. You got a map for spotting nervous system imbalance, with real-life clues and symptom checklists. We talked about preparing a safe space and making every practice adaptable, whether you live with trauma, chronic illness, or just a busy life.

You learned the science behind vagus nerve activation, minus the jargon. You discovered quick, practical exercises—such as breathing, humming, cold exposure, and self-massage—that fit into the messiness of real life.

From there, you began building simple daily rhythms—morning practices, small moments of calm during the day, and gentle wind-downs at night—while paying attention to what helped and adjusting your routine when life changed.

We discussed setbacks openly, along with gentle troubleshooting and ways to keep going even when you feel busy, tired, or discouraged.

You explored how to combine these tools with therapy, medication, or other healing paths. You also learned to celebrate small wins and begin rebuilding trust in your body.

Finally, you saw how nutrition, journaling, movement, and community support can all work together to create a more holistic approach to healing.

So, what are the big takeaways?

First, your vagus nerve is a powerful ally. You don't need to be perfect, and you don't need to do it all. Small, simple practices—done with intention and kindness—create real, lasting change. People don't need easy lives or smooth histories to heal. It's for all of us, no matter what we've been through. Setbacks are normal.

They don't mean you're broken or failing. They're just part of how the body relearns safety. Personalizing your routines is the key—your healing will look different than anyone else's, and that's precisely how it should be.

Please don't underestimate the work you've done. Even showing up for yourself in small ways—such as trying a breathing exercise, tracking your symptoms, or pausing to notice your body—takes bravery.

Healing isn't just about feeling better. It's about building a relationship with yourself based on respect, patience, and hope. If you've skipped days, struggled with routines, or doubted yourself along the way, you're not alone. The people who heal most deeply aren't the ones who do everything perfectly, but the ones who keep returning—with gentle persistence—to what helps.

Remember, this is a lifelong journey. The nervous system learns best through regular, repeated signals of safety and security. That might mean five minutes in the morning, a humming break during a stressful day, or a bedtime routine that signals "rest" instead of "alarm." Even if you only do a little, doing it regularly matters far more than doing it perfectly. Over time, these small choices build resilience, calm, and a sense of wellness you can trust.

As you move forward, I invite you to revisit your trackers. Notice what's working and what's not. Adjust your routines as your needs shift. Try out new exercises, or return to old favorites when life gets overwhelming. Keep updating your resilience toolkit—add tools that work, and let go of those that don't. Healing is never a straight line, and your needs will change over time, with stress, the seasons, and life events.

You don't have to do this alone. If you can, reach out to supportive communities—online groups, friends, therapy, or even just one caring person. Talk about your progress, your struggles, and your wins. Let others cheer for you (and, when needed, let them remind you that you're not alone). Ask for help when you need it—there's real strength in connection and accountability.

I designed this book to be different—trauma-sensitive, practical, and built for real life. You can adapt every exercise and make every step your own. Whether you're living with chronic illness, trauma, or a demanding schedule, you belong here. You deserve care that meets you exactly where you are.

Thank you for letting me walk this part of your journey with you. As a nurse and someone who cares deeply about genuine healing, it has been an honor to offer these tools and stories. I hope they help you reclaim calm, health, and joy—not just as ideas, but as lived experiences, day by day.

Before you close this book, I have one last invitation. Take one action today. Maybe you'll choose your favorite exercise and do it now. Perhaps you'll set up a daily routine, jot a note in your tracker, or pause to celebrate one small win. Whatever it is, let it be a gentle signal to your body: "I am here. I am healing. This is my next step."

No matter where life takes you next, I hope you'll return to these tools and reminders whenever you need them. You are resilient. You are worthy of calm and wellness. And you are never alone.

Make a Difference with Your Review

If any part of this book helped you feel a little more at ease in your body, or gave you a new way to relate to your pain, I'd be grateful to hear about it. Readers often rely on honest reviews to decide whether a book like this might be right for them.

If you feel comfortable sharing, you might mention what stood out to you or how the practices fit into your day. Even a few words can help someone else who's looking for gentle support.

You can leave a review on Amazon if you'd like to share your experience.

Thank you for showing up for yourself and for listening to your body.
—Hector Rivera, RN, BSN

Make a Difference with Your Review

References

- *Vagus Nerve: What It Is, Function, Location & Conditions* https://my.clevelandclinic.org/health/body/22279-vagus-nerve#:~:text=What%20is%20th e%20Vagus%20Nerve,can't%20consciously%20control%20them.
- *What is Polyvagal Theory?* https://www.polyvagalinstitute.org/whatispolyvagaltheory
- *The Vagus Nerve at the Interface of the Microbiota-Gut- ...*

HTTPS://WWW.FRONTIERSIN.ORG/JOURNALS/NEUROSCIENCE/ARTICLES/10.3389/FNINS.2018.00049/FULL

- *Resetting the Hype Around the Vagus Nerve* https://www.mcgill.ca/oss/article/critical-thinking/resetting-hype-around-vagus-nerve
- *Vagus Nerve: What It Is, Function, Location & Conditions* https://my.clevelandclinic.org/health/body/22279-vagus-nerve
- *Polyvagal Theory and How Trauma Impacts the Body* https://www.nicabm.com/trauma-polyvagal-theory-and-how-trauma-impacts-the-body/

- *Vagus Nerve Stimulation at the Interface of Brain–Gut ...*

https://pmc.ncbi.nlm.nih.gov/articles/PMC6671930/

- *Nervous System Dysregulation Assessment* https://healyournervoussystem.com/assessment/
- *18 Polyvagal Theory & How to Use the Exercises in Therapy* https://positivepsychology.com/polyvagal-theory/
- *How to regulate your nervous system and restore calm* https://www.calm.com/blog/how-to-regulate-nervous-system#:~:text=Rebalancing%20yo ur%20nervous%20system%20means,you%20trust%20can%20also%20help.
- *6 Vagus Nerve Exercises to Boost Your Well-being* https://yogauonline.com/yoga-practice-teaching-tips/yoga-practice-tips/6-ways-to-stimula te-your-vagus-nerve-with-yoga-and-breathing/
- *30 Grounding Techniques to Quiet Distressing Thoughts* https://www.healthline.com/health/grounding-techniques
- *Vagus Nerve as Modulator of the Brain–Gut Axis in ...* https://pmc.ncbi.nlm.nih.gov/articles/PMC5859128/
- *Study: PTSD Patients Show Long-Term Benefits with Vagus ...* https://news.utdallas.edu/health-medicine/study-ptsd-vagus-nerve-stimulation-2025/#:~:text=In%20a%20first%2Dof%2Dits,vagus%20nerve%20stimulation%20(VNS).

- *Assessing the therapeutic potential of vagus nerve ...* https://pmc.ncbi.nlm.nih.gov/articles/PMC11793006/

- *7 Ways to Support the Vagus Nerve and Improve Heart ...* https://www.larabriden.com/the-soothing-vagus-nerve/

- *Diaphragmatic Breathing Exercises and Your Vagus Nerve* https://www.psychologytoday.com/us/blog/the-athletes-way/201705/diaphragmatic-breat hing-exercises-and-your-vagus-nerve

- *The Power of Humming | Psychology Today* https://www.psychologytoday.com/us/blog/the-compassionate-brain/202410/the-power-of-humming#:~:text=Humming%20does%20more%20than%20create,fight%2Dor%2Dflight %20response.

- *Vagus Nerve Exercises - Charlie Health* https://www.charliehealth.com/post/vagus-nerve-exercises#:~:text=While%20engaging%

20in%20cold%20exposure,Doing%20a%20cold%20plunge

- *Vagus Nerve Massage: How to Stimulate the ...* https://drbrighten.com/vagus-nerve-massage/

- *5 Ways To Stimulate Your Vagus Nerve* https://health.clevelandclinic.org/vagus-nerve-stimulation

- *Relaxation Techniques - StatPearls* https://www.ncbi.nlm.nih.gov/books/NBK513238/

- *The Best Vagus Nerve Exercises for Better Sleep* https://www.charliehealth.com/areas-of-care/anxiety/vagus-nerve-exercises-for-sleep

- *5 Vagus Nerve Exercises to Help You Chill Out* https://www.charliehealth.com/post/vagus-nerve-exercises

- *The Vagus Nerve: Exercises for Calmness and Connection* https://fullyfunctional.com/blog/vagus-nerve/

- *Stimulate the vagus nerve & reduce stress with simple exercises* https://www.css.ch/en/private-customers/my-health/physical-health/stomach-digestion/sti mulate-vagus-nerve.html

- *Synergistic effects of vagus nerve stimulation and ...* https://pmc.ncbi.nlm.nih.gov/articles/PMC10511567/

- *Why Small Wins in Trauma Therapy Matter More Than You ...*

https://northvalleytherapy.org/why-small-wins-in-trauma-therapy-matter-more-than-you-th ink/

- *6 Vagus Nerve Exercises to Boost Your Well-being* https://yogauonline.com/yoga-practice-teaching-tips/yoga-practice-tips/6-ways-to-stimula te-your-vagus-nerve-with-yoga-and-breathing/

- *7 Wearable HRV Biofeedback Devices For Reducing Stress* https://www.diygenius.com/hrv-biofeedback-training/

- *Are you leading body scans in a trauma-informed way?*

https://www.softpathhealing.com/writing/are-you-leading-body-scans-in-a-trauma-informe d-way

- *18 Polyvagal Theory & How to Use the Exercises in Therapy* https://positivepsychology.com/polyvagal-theory/
- *5 Vagus Nerve Exercises to Help You Chill Out* https://www.charliehealth.com/post/vagus-nerve-exercises
- *Vagus nerve stimulation* https://www.mayoclinic.org/tests-procedures/vagus-nerve-stimulation/about/pac-2038456 5
- *Building a Support System - Trauma Informed* https://trauma-informed.ca/recovery/phases-of-trauma-recovery/building-a-support-syste m/
- *The Ultimate Guide to Self-Care While Traveling* https://traveltowellbeing.com/self-care-while-traveling-guide
- *Linking the Vagus Nerve and Gut Health* https://wisemindnutrition.com/blog/linking-vagus-nerve-gut-health
- *Online Positive Affect Journaling in the Improvement ...* https://pmc.ncbi.nlm.nih.gov/articles/PMC6305886/
- *The Resilience Toolkit Training Alliance* https://theresiliencetoolkit.co/
- *Book Club Study Guide: The Body Keeps the Score* https://traumaresearchfoundation.org/wp-content/uploads/2022/01/Book-Club-Study-Gui de_compressed.pdf

Other Books by Hector Rivera That May Support Your Healing

Somatic Exercises for Beginners

A clear and approachable starting point for anyone new to somatic work. This book introduces simple, body-based practices that help calm the nervous system, reduce overwhelm, and reconnect you with a sense of safety. You'll find easy exercises you can use throughout the day—no special setup or experience needed—along with guidance to help you build consistency without pressure.

Somatic Exercises for Trauma Healing

Gentle, body-based practices to help you reconnect with a sense of safety after trauma. This book focuses on small, manageable exercises that support your nervous system without overwhelm, helping you build trust with your body at a pace that feels right for you.

Somatic Exercises for Anxiety

This book focuses on practical techniques to help quiet racing thoughts, ease physical tension, and support a more stable emotional state. It walks you through short, manageable exercises you can use in real-life moments—at work, at home, or during stressful situations—so you can respond with more calm rather than feel stuck in cycles of worry.

Somatic Exercises for Chronic Pain

Designed for those living with ongoing discomfort, this book offers gentle, accessible practices to help reduce tension, improve body awareness, and support gradual relief. This book helps you work with your body rather than push through pain, with simple routines you can adapt to your energy level and daily life.

Author Bio

Hector Rivera, RN, BSN, is a nurse and author focused on practical, body-based approaches to healing. Drawing from both clinical experience and personal insight, his work centers on helping people understand how the nervous system influences stress, pain, sleep, and emotional well-being.

Through his somatic book series, Hector shares simple, accessible tools for everyday life—without pressure or complicated routines. His approach emphasizes working with the body, building consistency over time, and creating a sense of safety that supports lasting change.

He is the founder of HARZ Publishing, where he develops resources designed to make healing feel more approachable and realistic for people navigating anxiety, trauma, chronic pain, and burnout.

www.ingramcontent.com/pod-product-compliance
Lightning Source LLC
LaVergne TN
LVHW050958080826
845145LV00009B/2342

* 9 7 8 1 9 6 9 5 7 7 2 6 0 *